A Connected Life
Mystical Christianity for Today

Michael J Cunningham SDB

Graphics by Val O'Brien

CREDITS

Most Scripture quotations are from the New Revised Standard Version Bible, copyright © 1989 the Division of Christian Education of the National Council of the Churches of Christ in the United States of America. Used by permission. All rights reserved.
For some quotations *The Message* text is used, published by NavPress Publishing Group.

A Connected Life
Mystical Christianity for Today
© 2014
ISBN NO 9781909080294

Published by
Don Bosco Publications
Thornleigh House
Sharples Park
BOLTON BL1 6PQ
www.don-bosco-publications.co.uk
sarah@salesians.org.uk

Fonts used
Main text Calibri 12
Headings **Cambria Bold 16**
Quotes Minion Pro 12

Printed by
Buxton Press Limited
Palace Road, Buxton, Derbyshire, SK17 6AE

Dedication

This book is being published on the 40th anniversary of my ordination, years in which I have been richly blessed. I want to thank my family, my fellow Salesians, Salesian Sisters, other religious, laity and young people both here in the UK and in many parts of the world for sharing the journey with me.

Michael

Front Cover Graphic

Starry Night, Vincent van Gogh's famous painting, is renowned for its bold whorls of light sweeping across a raging night sky. Although this image of the heavens came only from the artist's restless imagination, a picture from the Hubble Space Telescope bears remarkable similarities to the van Gogh work, complete with never-before-seen spirals of dust swirling across trillions of kilometres of interstellar space.

This image, obtained with the Advanced Camera for Surveys on 8th February, 2004, is Hubble's view of an expanding halo of light around a distant star, named V838 Monocerotis (V838 Mon). The illumination of interstellar dust comes from the red supergiant star at the middle of the image, giving off a flashbulb-like pulse of light. V838 Mon is located about 20,000 light-years away from Earth in the direction of the constellation Monoceros, placing the star at the outer edge of our Milky Way galaxy.

Credit:
NASA (National Aeronautics and Space Administration)
the Hubble Heritage Team
and ESA (European Space Agency)

Contents

Foreword	6
Introduction	8
1. Beyond a Superficial Life	12
2. An Enticing Mystery	23
3. Seeing with a Contemplative Heart	33
4. Lights-On Mysticism	43
5. Lights-Off Mysticism	53
6. Beyond yet Intimate	64
7. The Jesus Revolution	74
8. The Mystery of Paradox	87
9. One with Creation	97
10. A Relational God	108

Foreword

Life, of its nature, is dynamic. We are never finished growing. However, the process of growth is not straight forward. The psychologist Erik Erikson, in his theory of psychosocial development, says that we go through eight stages of growth from childhood to old age. In each stage there is a conflict which enables us to develop a psychological quality or fail to develop that quality. In each stage the possibility for growth is great and so is the possibility for failure. Therefore, our growth can get stuck or hindered along the way and sometimes we are not even aware of it.

Similarly, in our faith journey there are stages we must pass through to reach a mature faith. James Fowler posits a six stage theory of faith development. However, he claims that many people remain stuck in stage three. In this stage we become dependent solely on external authority and fail to internalise our beliefs. As a result we become stuck in a particular *theological box* and there is the danger of viewing reality through a very narrow lens where everything is black or white, right or wrong, good or bad. Our seeing may become very blinkered, biased and judgemental leaving little room for paradox and mystery and for the brokenness and messiness of life.

Fr Michael Cunningham's insightful and timely book maps out a different way of seeing, tracing a more life-giving path for our spiritual journey. In a very accessible and readable manner he gradually uncovers for us again one of the richest traditions of our Church – the contemplative, mystical tradition. In doing so, he very ably highlights how the contemplative perspective can become a lived reality for all of us in our daily lives. It is not just a way of life for the chosen few.

One of the great Catholic theologians, Karl Rahner, famously wrote, back in the 1950s:

> The Christian of the future will either be a *mystic*, one who has experienced *something*, or he will cease to be anything at all.

Fr Michael's reflections are in the same vein and he helps us to further discover the wisdom and depth of Rahner's assertion. Perhaps, Rahner himself did not realise how far-seeing his words were when he wrote them over half a century ago. Undoubtedly, he expressed a profound intuition as well as an ability to read the signs of the times. Since then there has been a massive disenchantment with institutional religion and people have moved from a culture of authority to a culture of experience.

Fr Michael shows how our largely-forgotten tradition is in tune with the spiritual hungers of our own time. The mystical and contemplative tradition always gave due credence to personal experience as well as to external authority.

The other great contribution that this book makes is that it helps us to become more familiar and less frightened of words like *mystic, mysticism, meditation* and *contemplation*. He situates these words and concepts in the heart of our Christian tradition. In doing so he shows the wisdom and beauty of this tradition. By reminding us that the mystical path, contemplative prayer and meditation are an intrinsic part of our tradition, he lays to rest the myth that these are merely some New Age invention.

This book is to be warmly welcomed by anybody wishing to explore further the richness and wisdom of an active-contemplative approach to life.

John Horan SDB
Ash Wednesday 2014

Introduction

> What I say to you I say to all: Keep awake.
>
> Mark 13:37

There is, in all of us, a homing device that calls us to our deepest centre, the core of our being, what we call the soul. As Christians we have traditionally been told that we are here on this earth to save our souls. Spiritual teachers today are using a different language. They speak of finding our soul or growing our soul rather than saving it. Carl Jung famously remarked that modern man is in search of his soul, and I think this accurately describes the hunger and longing for something more that so many people feel today.

It is not easy to define the word *soul*; in fact it is impossible but there are times in our lives when we feel the need to connect with this spiritual centre of our being. This is what I am trying to describe in this short book. I am not an original thinker but I have tried, however inadequately, to point to some of the exciting writers who are exploring this territory. What is commonly agreed is that there is a profound experience of connection at the core of our being. This has always been the case. Today we are witnessing a revolution in human experience.

There is much interest these days in the idea of development. Teachers such as Jean Piaget, James Fowler, Carol Gilligan, Ken Wilber, Don Beck, Lawrence Kohlberg, Bill Plotkin and Richard Rohr are all concerned with mapping out the growth of human consciousness which is at the heart of the revolution of our times. They all have their different nuances and emphases but the crucial point of agreement is that lower levels of consciousness are inevitably dualistic, whereas the higher levels move towards non-dual or unitive consciousness.

Our Christian myth of the Fall taught us that Adam and Eve enjoyed a kind of unitive consciousness as they walked and conversed with God in the cool of the evening in the garden of Eden. It was an experience of innocence. The Fall occurred when they sought the knowledge of good and evil. In a sense this was a necessary step in the growth of consciousness into the rational, analytic mind that could separate and discriminate. The price was to move from unitive consciousness into divided consciousness, from oneness with creation to separateness. So emerged the myth of the strong, individual, autonomous self, whose identity could be found in power and possessions. This is still the predominant myth that shapes most people's lives today. It is the underlying cause of much of the conflict, violence and unhappiness that we experience in our world today. The collapse of the world's banking systems has laid bare the inadequacy of the myth that the rational mind alone can deliver happiness.

Institutional religion has not been much help in recent centuries. It too has adopted the masculine path of rational thinking. At the same time the real heart of religion and spirituality, the way of wisdom, has been neglected. The most evident sign of this has been the neglect of the mystical path and contemplative prayer. Much of our religious teaching and preaching has been locked into the either/or of the dualistic mind rather than the more inclusive both/and of the wisdom tradition favoured by the mystics. Where the Jesus of the gospels is revealed as an inclusive non-dual, non-violent lover of the poor and of sinners, the Church has often clothed itself as hierarchical, masculine, judgemental and clerical. Happily we now have a Pope who is urging us to rediscover the joy of the gospel and the mercy of God.

Non-dual thinking opens us up to a new way of seeing. This is the particular gift of meditation and contemplative prayer. Contemplation is not just about prayer; it is new way of seeing. It perceives oneness before it perceives division. It doesn't ignore diversity – in fact it celebrates it – but it places it within the deeper reality where everything is connected.

We live in a period of time when global connection is a fact as well as a dream. We are connected electronically, economically and politically. But if we neglect the deepest connection at the level of our souls – that we are one with God, one with others, and one with creation – our technical connections alone will not satisfy our deepest longings and hunger.

Science, technology and religion need to come together. The discoveries of quantum physics regarding the universe we inhabit are revolutionising the way we understand ourselves. The static view of Isaac Newton's world, which views every aspect of the universe as disconnected, has given way to the astonishing view that the whole universe is a vast web of interconnection. From the microcosm to the macrocosm, the smallest to the largest, everything is relational and this profound scientific view is helping us to rediscover a much richer understanding of God. We see God as a relational mystery of intimacy and communion, not the static unchanging old man in the sky. We are not outside this mystery but drawn into it by Jesus who is the Christ through whom everything has been made and in whom everything is being brought together.

We are living in an evolutionary universe. As we marvel at the photographs of our planet from space and the wonders revealed by the Hubble telescope, we discover ourselves to be the conscious part of evolution. The challenge before us is immense. Are we prepared to enter in and participate in the emergence of God-centred love and creativity that is the unfolding of the body of Christ? Or are we content to live at a superficial level as *we amuse ourselves to death* in Neil Postman's vivid phrase?

We find ourselves today at the beginning of a new axial age. Life in our universe is a mystery of participation, what Thomas Merton called the cosmic dance. The first axial age, from 800 to 200 BC, witnessed the emergence of all the great religions and the rational individual. The awareness of our deep connection with all life is at the heart of the coming second axial age and in a growing sense that to be human is to share in a mystery of participation.

In the past we found God in stone temples, sacred places and cathedrals. Now we find God in the depths of our hearts and souls, we are rediscovering the unified consciousness that breaks the division of sacred and secular, body and soul, matter and spirit, heaven and earth, as our new way of seeing reveals everything as it is: an infinite mystery of unity in diversity.

1. Beyond a Superficial Life

I am rather close to the mystical movement.
Pope Francis

Towards the end of his life Albert Einstein was asked if he had any regrets. He said that he wished he had read more of the mystics. This is a very interesting statement from a man whose work in many ways ushered in the postmodern world and consciousness. We have become a global village and the change is so wide-reaching and fast that we haven't really caught up with it yet. The early years of the twenty first century have already witnessed the collapse of the banking systems with effects right across the globe, and the acknowledgment by the world's scientists that ninety five per cent of global warming is man-made. The technological revolution in means of communication has brought us all closer together, and while celebrity culture is paraded before our eyes as entertainment, we cannot escape the horrific images of war, violence and acts of terrorism in many parts of the world. Political leaders and global institutions struggle to react to the pace of change.

I recall the news pictures of a deeply traumatised young boy in Syria who was suffering with forty-degree burns. As he described his agony, he asked, *Why do they attack us with bombs when we are in school?* He is simply one of thousands of children who were innocent victims of a brutal civil war which has created over two million refugees. I remember the terrified faces of children being carried by their mothers to escape the merciless violence of Al-Shabaab terrorists in Nairobi. Across the USA and in Europe there seems to be an increasing fear of the foreigner, the stranger, the other. The fall of the Berlin Wall was one of the most hopeful signs of the twentieth century; now in the twenty first century we have witnessed the building of walls to separate Jews from Arabs, and Latinos from Americans. As the world gets smaller we seem to be building walls in our hearts between nations, races and religions.

However our media can bring us good news stories. We, in Britain, shared the spontaneous joy of the Olympic Games in London and celebrated the wonderful generosity of so many volunteers who welcomed and assisted visitors from all parts of the world. In an often violent world we need to see the basic goodness of ordinary people. Everyone asked how we could sustain the *Olympic Spirit* but of course it inevitably fades once the event is over. There are many heart-warming stories of individual kindness and service to others, some reported by our media, many others unreported.

We are in a world in transition in which many traditional ways of behaving and thinking are being left behind and this has created great uncertainty and anxiety. We inhabit a technologically-connected global village; but we lack a global spirituality that allows us to recognise and celebrate our common humanity. Our lives seem to swing between optimism and fear. The response of the Catholic Church to our contemporary world has been severely weakened by the scandals of clerical sexual abuse and the disastrous cover-up by the hierarchy in many parts of the world. This has done and continues to do great harm to the Church's credibility. It will take many years to overcome but, while the credibility of the Church remains damaged, there are some positive signs emerging. We have the election of a new Pope who is able to reach out to the poor and warm the hearts of the faithful. Pope Francis is a man who is not only imbued with the Spirit, but is one who can communicate God's unconditional love and mercy in simple words and images.

Another very positive sign is the growing emergence of the mystical heart of Christianity. I write as a Catholic priest who has celebrated 40 years of priesthood, and as a Salesian of Don Bosco who will soon celebrate 50 years of profession. In my early years of formation and training there was no mention of mysticism, nor of the contemplative path. When it came to prayer-time everything came out of the *kataphatic* box of spirituality which uses words, images, thoughts, feelings and includes the Eucharist, the Prayer of the Church, the rosary, devotions and so on. These are all good and worthy ways of praying but there is another more radical path. The path of what is called *apophatic* spirituality – beyond words, thoughts, and images – has remained closed for almost all of the last four or five hundred years. I am beginning this book on the feast of one of the most popular saints in the Catholic Church, Saint Thérèse of Lisieux, whose life still has great import for our times. In the judgement of Father Thomas Keating she was one of the key figures in the revival of the contemplative dimension of the gospel, which is beginning to spread across the world.

For the last five centuries mysticism and mystics have been largely ignored, even classed as rather weird or dangerous. Both the Reformation and the Enlightenment chose reason and science as the only tools to discover truth. This was particularly disastrous for Western Christianity because it meant that we no longer looked at the world with the eyes of Jesus. It led to the centuries of individualism and separatism that has characterised Western culture. None of us is immune from this way of looking at reality.

But the Spirit is clearly moving in our world and there are signs that we are on the verge of a new kind of consciousness as we struggle to live fully human lives in these challenging times, and we Christians have a unique contribution to make.

We hear a lot about *new evangelisation*, this cannot just mean proselytising, but rather the creation of a new kind of *consciousness,* one that moves us beyond our egocentric separatism to a sense of oneness. A consciousness that fits the challenges that are emerging in our times.

Beyond Entertainment

If there is one word that characterises the mood of our times I would suggest it is *disenchantment*. It appears that rejection of God is the default position for most educated people today. It was the sociologist Max Weber who used this term to describe how modern people view the world. We are on our own and we cannot rely on God for any assistance. Everything is subject to our own rational management. The world is there to be mastered and controlled by our own effort and will-power, not wondered at or celebrated. This is a negative but, I suggest, an accurate reading of what seems to be happening. However, within this place of indifference to religion there is a growing interest in spirituality. Why is this?

We know that our egos seek to provide us with as much control as possible over our lives. So much of our technology today seeks to empower this kind of egocentric living. Television companies provide us with all kinds of techniques for recording programmes that we may have missed, watching them when we want; the whole package is based on me watching what I want when I want it. With endless digital channels, smart phones, MP3 players and so on we have become the most entertained culture in human history. How could we ever be bored? And yet we are, maybe more than we care to admit. As soon as a new phone appears on the market, people rush to buy. Once possessed it is out of date as the next piece of technical wizardry comes along.

Some years ago I bought a copy of the book *Amusing Ourselves to Death* by Neil Postman. Unfortunately I have since lost my copy but I recall what Postman was saying in the 1980s. He argued that much of our public discourse, journalism, education, and even religion is packaged as entertainment. Postman contrasted George Orwell's vision in his chilling book *1984* with Aldous Huxley's *Brave New World*. Orwell had warned against external oppression that would take away freedom; Huxley warned that we would welcome our freedom being taken away by our technologies and embrace the superficial life.

Technology is not bad; it is a tool that we all like to use. I much prefer to be typing these words on a laptop rather than, as have would have been the case a few years back, with a typewriter. The problem is that it comes with a price. It tends to keep us on the surface of our lives to the neglect of our inner being, what we have always called our souls. The purpose of this book is to promote the contemplative path which the mystics travel upon and invite us to follow their courageous journey as explorers of the soul. It is a path that searches for hidden wholeness rather than external forms. It is a path that seeks union with Ultimate Reality, what many religions call God, rather than what lies on the surface of reality. It is not an easy path but it provides a response to the widespread spiritual hunger of our times. It is a path that others cannot walk for us; we must walk it ourselves.

Spirituality as Transformation

Western Christianity still hasn't fully resolved the tension that created the Reformation. Protestants emphasised the importance of scripture (sola scriptura) while Catholics clung on to the importance of tradition (papacy and hierarchy). What lost out in this clash was personal experience. The Reformation was so caught up in dualism that each side was prepared to torture and kill in the name of Christ. We seem to forget that Jesus read the scriptures through the prism of his own inner experience of God. He had the courage to challenge the so-called experts on the Law as he drew on his own experience of his loving Father. He took the scriptures seriously but not literally. He moved beyond the letter of the law to uncover its deeper meaning: *You have heard it said..... but I say to you*. In this he revealed himself as a wisdom teacher.

The scriptures have been described by Rene Girard as a *text in travail*. They are a record of a people's attempts to understand God and live accordingly. At times they provide passages of high-level consciousness, and at others very low-level consciousness, which shows how dangerous fundamentalism is in taking the texts literally. Do we really believe that God told his people to slaughter all their enemies when they entered the Promised Land? Do we really believe that God wants us to pluck out our eyes or cut off our hands when we sin? The books of scripture can be read at so many levels and their true richness is revealed in the light of our personal experience of God. Jesus shows us how to do this when we see him in the gospels moving beyond exclusivism to inclusivism, from punishment to forgiveness, from literalism to mercy. What gave him this wisdom? It was his rich inner experience of God as *Abba*, his loving father. So often we read of him going off into the hills to pray.

When we look at the scriptures in this way we begin to discern a clear pattern of religious development, a path of spiritual transformation, from Law through Prophets to Wisdom.

We all have to start where the Jewish scriptures begin, with the Torah: the Law. It provides a structure, rules and regulations, traditions and rituals that give the ego a foundational security of certainty, identity, order and authority. Today too many children in our postmodern culture lack this foundation. They are left as the centre of their own world, free to choose whatever they want. They are the children of the entitlement culture. It inflates the ego in a dangerous way that makes the give-and-take of mature relationships problematic. The necessary stage of the Law is often missing. A healthy upbringing supplies a container in which we can grow, guided by the outer authority of parents, teachers and wise elders. The emphasis is on control and conformity. It is a hierarchical, patriarchal, top-down system. Sadly a lot of contemporary religion stays at this level, which is why many adults leave the institutional Church. We hear of no other path.

One of the most serious problems with this first-half-of-life spirituality is that it *privatises* the spiritual path. It reduces religion to a personal plan of salvation which shifts the emphasis from living a fuller life in this world to trying to get into heaven. It leads to performance-based religion which reduces God to a driving instructor who notes every right and wrong action and punishes us accordingly.

What leads us beyond this rather immature stage is revealed in the scriptures by the prophets. It remains the least quoted and most ignored part of the scriptures. The prophets point to the basic flaw in the human condition: that none of us can achieve perfection. Human experience includes the tragic and the imperfect. We are all wounded. The prophets teach us about the dark as well as the light. They move us to the vital stage of self-critical thinking. They are loyal critics of religion who live in the most difficult place, both inside and on the edge of tradition. What gives them authority to criticise the status quo is the fact that they are in touch with their inner selves, the God within. In a word they are mystics, and mystics are often perceived as threats. Jesus referred to this when he pointed out how so many of them were killed. Sadly the Christian Church has often ignored and side-lined the mystics. Very few of them are canonised; others, such as Meister Eckhart, were condemned by Church authority.

It has to be admitted that those who rely on inner authority to the exclusion of outer authority can sometimes tread dangerous waters. In recent history our Western culture has largely moved away from the conservative containers of the post-war world in the 1960s. At the time the cry was to throw off all restrictions in a heady rush towards freedom and personal liberty. All authorities were questioned. All attempts at an explanation, a big picture of meaning – which inevitably includes religion – were swept away in what has become known today as postmodernism. Ideas of the common good, of our common sense of belonging, were left behind in the search for personal authenticity. But this too was a necessary stage of growth, an emerging from group adolescence.

The genius of the scriptures is to point a way through the impasse between outer and inner authority. This is the Wisdom Tradition which invites us to move into the second stage of life. Here we are able to respect both outer and inner authority and move towards a deeper synthesis. The Wisdom books include the book of Job, Proverbs, Ecclesiastes and some of the psalms, and the Song of Songs. This is the stage of non-dual thinking which should be the goal of all mature religion. The Book of Job pushes us towards the contemplative way of living and seeing. The law-abiding good man asks God why he has to suffer so much. It is so unjust. God's answer to Job is to remind him of their relationship, which can enfold even the mystery of suffering and not be crushed by it.

While the first-half-of-life religion chooses light over dark, the second stage moves us into a more spacious field where light and dark can be held in creative tension. It points to the figure of Jesus. It moves us to the mature level of a relational spirituality. Jesus called it The Kingdom of God. It allows us to include rather than exclude all of reality, light and dark, and transform it by the wine of compassion, forgiveness, mercy and love. In John's gospel we hear of the woman who had committed adultery. The scribes and Pharisees, secure in the legalism of the Law, think they have cornered Jesus. The Law states that the woman should be stoned to death and they ask Jesus what he thinks. It is black and white. Jesus writes in the ground and then asks a question straight out of the prophetic awareness of our common woundedness: he asks anyone who thinks he is sinless to throw the first stone. Here we see Jesus moving us into the area of paradox and ambiguity, beyond a simplistic black and white judgement. As they all drift away Jesus refuses to condemn the woman but he challenges her to change the way she has been living. That is wisdom teaching.

The prophetic call is a summons to hold the pain and evil in the world and to transform it into forgiveness. We cannot do this on our own. Mysticism helps us to confront the evil within ourselves as we open ourselves to the unconditional love of God. We receive forgiveness and learn how to pass it on to others, because that is what God does to us. We awaken to the connected life. What is done to us is what we must do to others.

Wisdom teaching invites us to live out of non-dual consciousness, unitive consciousness, union with God and thereby to move beyond the simple dualisms of right and wrong, good and bad, knowing and not knowing. This is spirituality as transformation and is the work of the Holy Spirit. In the biblical pattern the movement is from simple consciousness through to complex consciousness and on to an enlightened consciousness. In simple consciousness we are still drawn all too easily into splitting, dividing, comparing and judging. We dismiss the darkness and identify too easily with the light. In enlightened consciousness we are able to include rather than exclude both the light and the dark. In contemplative prayer we experience God's forgiveness of our own darkness and learn how to forgive the darkness in others.

This is not an easy step and it will be resisted by our egos. This is why Jesus tells us that something has to die if we are to discover and learn how to live inside our true selves. The task for the second half is to move beyond fragmentation into wholeness, and to discover the connection between the outer and inner dimensions of our life. As followers of Jesus we are called to create a more just world, but if we are to create such a world we must also face the inner journey into our souls. We can't really change or convert anyone else. We can only change ourselves.

This is where the mystics begin to teach us. Modern psychology has given us a language to look into the unconscious and discover what truly motivates us. Centuries ago, mystics such as Teresa of Ávila and John of the Cross were describing these blockages to growth. They didn't have the language we use today but John of the Cross spoke of the dark night of the soul, teaching which is still relevant in the spiritual life today. Teresa of Ávila described the soul as an interior castle with many rooms, and the starting point of the journey to wholeness was always humble self-knowledge.

In the gospels we see Jesus engaged in teaching and healing. Catholics have often focussed on Jesus as a moral teacher, and that clearly fits into the task of the first half of life.

We paid little attention to the healing ministry, perhaps because of the language used by the gospel writers. We often read of Jesus casting out demons; in the first chapter of Mark's gospel there are four references to demons. In our sophisticated Western culture we are inclined to dismiss these stories. Our contemporary demons are our everyday addictions, which are primarily relational and psychological. One of our strongest addictions is to our own opinion, our own point of view.

The mystics invite us to walk the contemplative path as a road to healing where we can meet God not just as someone to believe in or to work hard for, but as the lover of our souls. This is the call to intimacy, for which all of us have been created. This is not an easy path; it involves some dying and, as we shall see in the next chapter, the Church itself, which should have been guiding us towards this path, has for too long ignored it.

2. An Enticing Mystery

> Highly ought we to rejoice that God dwellet in our soul, and much more highly ought we to rejoice that our soul dwelleth in God. Our soul is made to be God's dwelling place; and the dwelling place of the soul is God, Which is unmade.
>
> *Julian of Norwich*[1]

Contemplation was taught in the first fifteen centuries in the Western Church. Since that time it has long been ignored and it was only in the latter half of the twentieth century that it began to be revived. The widespread popularity of St Thérèse of Lisieux's autobiography, *The Story of a Soul,* and the writings of Thomas Merton began the revival. It has been greatly assisted by the work of *Contemplative Outreach* begun by Fr Thomas Keating and Fr William Menninger, and the *World Community for Christian Meditation* founded by the English Benedictine, Fr John Maine. This was continued after his death by Fr Lawrence Freeman. Richard Rohr also promotes contemplative prayer through his *Center for Action and Contemplation* in Albuquerque, New Mexico, and there are other notable teachers such as Cynthia Bourgeault, James Finlay, Bede Griffiths, Tilden Edwards, Carl McColman and the Carmelite, Ruth Burrows. What is particularly noteworthy is that these contemporary teachers are reaching out to lay people as well as priests and members of religious communities. I have been to conferences to listen to some of these gifted teachers and there are always large numbers of lay people attending. The hunger is clearly emerging in our times, as we swing between fear of global terrorism and love for our neighbour.

---

1. Julian of Norwich *Revelations of Divine Love* (Christian Classics Ethereal Library; 2009)

I once had a conversation with a young religious about prayer. He told me that during his novitiate he wanted to learn more about contemplative prayer. A priest told him not to go in that direction, just to stay with discursive meditation. I asked him who the priest was and he said it was his novice master. I wasn't too surprised to hear that because the revival of contemplation is still in its early stages. I doubt if many seminaries or houses of formation are teaching it. Thomas Keating[2] refers to the many founders of religious congregations in recent centuries who lived lives of union with God, but did not teach contemplation to their followers. I know this is true of my own founder, Don Bosco.[3] It takes a long time to recover this pearl of great price which was a hidden treasure for the last five hundred years or so.

As mentioned in Chapter One, we have been putting all our eggs into the basket of reason. It has been a necessary growth in consciousness and, along with science and technology, has produced many good things in our modern world. Nevertheless it has its limits. While reason is fine when trying to solve everyday problems, it cannot deal with mystery. It is no help at all with the great matters of life such as Love, Joy, Suffering, Death and Eternity. This is where the mystics entice us to follow them.

Hidden Treasure

The Infinite Love that we call God has fashioned our hearts in such a way that nothing less than Infinite Love will satisfy us. The simple message is that we have been made by Infinite Love to enjoy Infinite Love, our origin and the very ground of our being.

2. Thomas Keating, *Open Mind Open Heart* (Continuum, New York 1992 See chapter3)
3. Michael Cunningham, *Salesians, Contemplatives in Action* (Don Bosco Publications 2012)

Mystics such as Augustine, Julian of Norwich, Catherine of Genoa, Teresa of Ávila and John of the Cross all confidently state that God is closer to us than we are to ourselves. They are not proclaiming this as a doctrine to be accepted by the mind, but as a real experience of the heart that is open to all humanity. Too often we assume that this kind of experience is just for holy people like the saints. Sadly the Church herself took this view of mysticism in recent centuries leading to the side-lining of this wonderful path. However, John of the Cross makes it very clear that this invitation is open to everyone:

> To understand this union of which we speak, know that God is present in substance in each soul, even that of the greatest sinner in the world. And this kind of union with God always exists, in all creatures.[4]

Augustine said the same thing centuries earlier when he declared that God has made us for himself and until we begin to experience this union, our hearts will remain restless. We will spend eternity plunging deeper and deeper into this love, but the point the mystics make is that we can begin to experience it increasingly in this life. Why not start now?

This, in fact, is God's will for us. In the first half of life we tend to think of God's will as something that we have to do, a pattern of moral behaviour. We think that if we can pile up enough observances we will hopefully convince God to let us into heaven. For many Christians this is what religion is all about: believing the right doctrines, practising the right rituals and following the right commandments and moral prescriptions. This is performance-related religion. Despite Paul's teaching on grace in Romans and Galatians, it still exerts a strong pull on many Christians.

---

4. John of the Cross *The Ascent of Mt. Carmel*, Bk 2, Ch 5

The mystics point to a very different vision and way of living. They tell us that God's will is in fact himself. It is all about a relationship of love. God's love cannot be conditional on our behaviour; it is unconditional. Infinite Love has created us for infinite union. The more we realise this the more we desire to align ourselves with God's will in the way we live, which now involves doing the most loving action in every situation we meet. Mystical prayer doesn't take us away from the cares of the world; it immerses us right back into them because it changes the way we see and perceive reality. We begin to perceive oneness rather than the duality of the separate self.

The mystic is the one whose life is so transformed that he or she is one with God, one with everyone else and one with creation. We know from what the prophets tell us about our wounded condition that we cannot transform ourselves; it is the work of the Spirit. Our task is to let go of our egocentric way of looking at reality and discover our true identity in God. This is the True Self which is waiting to be awakened in the core of our being. Our True Self is the union in which we are sustained breath by breath, heartbeat by heartbeat. If we were not being sustained by Infinite Love, moment by moment, we would cease to exist. The letter to the Ephesians underlines how even before our physical birth we have always been in the mind of God:

> Long before he had laid down earth's foundations,
> he had us in mind, as the focus of his love, to be
> made whole and holy by his love.[5]

This deep union is our God-given godly nature and is the inherent sacredness of life itself, which includes the whole of created reality. This is why Francis of Assisi spoke of *Brother Sun* and *Sister Moon*, and Thomas Merton spoke of the cosmic dance.

---

5. Eph 1:4 *The Message* Eugene H Peterson (Nav Press Colorado Springs 2003)

It is all a mystery of participation and, rather than stand as wallflowers, we are all invited to join in the cosmic dance that – whether or not we realise it – *beats in our very blood*, in Merton's vivid phrase.⁶

In this different perspective we move from our separate individualistic lives to sharing in the deep connection that binds everything in unity. Spirituality is an awakening process. We are the finite manifestation of God's Infinite Love. Today we are beginning to understand that the whole of Creation is the manifestation of God's Infinite Love. From our evolutionary perspective on creation we discover ourselves as the consciousness of evolution. God's will becomes alive in us as we fulfil our destiny by allowing God's love to become ever more realised in our lives. What the mystics tell us is that only love is real. So what in the recent history of Western Christianity was seen as a limited option for a few special souls, is becoming central to the renewal of the Church in our globalised world.

Faith as Trust

For too long Catholics have been taught that faith means believing in the right doctrinal truths expressed in the correct verbal formula. We know that in the early centuries Christians struggled to find correct words. This was necessary as heretical views were in the air. Some accepted the divinity of Jesus but denied his humanity, while others accepted the humanity and denied his divinity. The Church took a strong both/and stance and, after many struggles, the Nicene and Apostles' Creeds were agreed upon. But these important and guiding statements that have stood the test of time cannot fully express what Jesus meant by faith. For him it is much more a matter of trust.

---

6. William H Shannon, Thomas Merton, *Thomas Merton's Paradise Journey: Writings on Contemplation* Continuum (1 Mar 2000) p 178

We see this in many of the gospel stories. In the second chapter of Mark's gospel we hear of the paralysed man being let down through the roof of a packed house where Jesus was teaching. Mark tells us that Jesus *saw their faith* and said to the paralysed man, *Your sins are forgiven* followed by, *Take up your bed and walk.* What was Jesus referring to when the gospel says, *he saw their faith*? There is no mention of doctrinal teachings. What he saw, and was impressed with, was their trust in the fact that he was a man of God, a man who was radiating the love of God as Father. In chapter seven of his gospel Luke relates the story of the *sinful* woman who entered the house of Simon the Pharisee and shocked all the men there by bathing and anointing the feet of Jesus in a very intimate way. In the face of male disapproval Jesus was touched by her faith, *Your faith has saved you, go in peace.* Again there is no evidence that this woman had taken any specific instructions in religious beliefs and doctrines.

There are so many examples like this in the gospels. What they tell us is that while doctrines provide a necessary shape to our beliefs, what is at the core of faith is a basic trust in the goodness and the compassion of the holy mystery that we call God. In the Catholic tradition too much emphasis was placed on the correct formula and doctrine. I remember at school learning catechism answers off by heart. We felt that this gave us a certainty that other religions did not have. This was particularly true in the post-reformation centuries. In the first thousand years of Christian history the theologian was *the one who prays*. Gradually this balance was lost. When the great schools of theology were founded in the 12th century they gradually followed the path of analytical thought and precision. This again was a necessary development of our rational minds but unfortunately it spilled over into the area of prayer and began to lose its contemplative roots.

The voices of the mystics were becoming lost and with that the vital message: that the mystery we call God cannot be defined and limited by words. We chose the kataphatic path and lost the apophatic. The Reformation was the high point of dualism, and we live with its consequences today with our many divisions in Christianity.

In eternity we will learn to love God in the way that Christ loves the Father and the Holy Spirit. We will see God face to face. Despite this incredibly enticing prospect we have to admit that we are often not very good at trusting this mystery, and while we want God to be on our side we don't want to let him get too close. We prefer acquaintance with God rather than friendship and intimacy. Most of our prayers are petitionary, asking God for favours. Thomas Merton used to say that we have a list of things to do and then when we get to the end of the list we will have more time for God, and the years go by and the list is still there. Yet with God there is no list.

When a blind man is told about the colour yellow he can have no experience of that colour. That is faith. It speaks to us about matters beyond human reason. All we have is the faith that there is a colour yellow. It is the same with our ideas and theological insights about God. Even when we say God is love, God is infinite, we are using metaphors for a mystery that transcends all these things. That is why God has given us Jesus so that the invisible God becomes visible in a human being.

Brokenness and Non-Duality

In Christ we see God's response to our forgetfulness, to our distraction, to our contentment with superficiality, to our workaholic lifestyle. Instead of rejection he identifies with us in our very brokenness, in our distraction, in our vulnerability.

What the mystics reveal is that each one of us is invincibly precious in the invincible love, all that is real. T S Eliot said, *Humankind cannot bear very much reality*, hence our settling for superficiality as our comfort zone. The real sadness of our lives is not that we slip and fall but that we give more authority to our brokenness than we give to the Infinite Love that loves us in our very brokenness. This is the good news: that God's Infinite Love sustains us and is continually being poured out into our broken lives as tenderness, as mercy, as compassion.

Love does not rest until there is an equality of love and it is in the nature of love to lift the beloved until there is equality. Mystics like John of the Cross proclaim that Infinite Love will not rest until you are equal in love to God. This is the goal of communion. We have the words of Jesus for this profound mystery:

> As you, Father, are in me and I am in you, may they also be in us. The glory that you have given me I have given them, so that they may be one, as we are one, I in them and you in me, that they may become completely one.[7]

It seems that God has decided that he will not wait until we are dead to begin this consummation of union. This is non-duality. We can say, *I am not God but I am not other than God. I am not you but I am not other than you. I am not the earth but I am not other than the earth.*

Awakening to non-dual thinking and seeing does not mean that you are holier than someone who is not aware. It is the gift that enables us to see how holy everybody is. Mystics are full of this vision and awareness. It allows us to see the world through the eyes of Jesus. We can begin to see the cosmic dance and participate actively in it. We learn how to

---
7. Jn 17:21-22

place our judging mind inside our heart which the mystics declare is the primary organ of perception. We see unity before duality and difference. We learn how to put the two together. Many of us struggle to believe this. We are stuck with our egocentric way of seeing reality. John of the Cross calls this our addiction to the finite in the perception that it is enough for us. We are afraid to go beyond the frontiers of our finiteness. Some give up the contemplative path because it asks them to let go of their thoughts and feelings. Their thoughts and feelings are their comfort zone. The contemplative path is the invitation to personal intimacy with Infinite Love, but God keeps calling and inviting, and waits humbly for our response.

There is still a common perception among believers, including priests and religious, that mysticism is somewhat esoteric and strange; not the normal path for ordinary people. We may think that being a mystic is to walk a path of certainty and clarity. In fact the opposite would be nearer the truth and is one of the reasons why I think that mysticism is more than ever needed in our contemporary world. What if the path of the mystic is one of dark as well as light?

The mystics lead us into the mystery of the Cloud of Unknowing and the Dark Night of the Soul. In Chapter One I described St Thérèse of Lisieux as one of the most popular saints of our time. Some might be inclined to dismiss the spirituality of this young French woman as soft and sentimental. Nothing could be further from the truth. Towards the end of her life Thérèse described her soul as being invaded by the thickest of darkness. This lasted up to her death when her experience of God was much more one of absence rather than consoling presence. It wasn't just a part of her spiritual life; it was the entirety of her spiritual life. She talked of a brick wall between herself and thoughts of heaven.

As she suffered both physically and spiritually she turned her whole life over to God in the purest faith and love. She knew that the danger of seeking consolation from God is to seek the feelings of consolation rather than God. She was prepared to accept the Infinite Love of God for her despite all the evidence of feeling.

I think the spirituality of the mystics is much needed in our world. We cannot live all the time at the level of non-dual thinking. We need to recognise duality as well as non-duality. It is a question of where we place our emphasis. The mystics teach us how to hold and live with the great paradoxes of life. Today our world of simple certainties has long gone as we find ourselves in a bewildering world of change. What mystics like Thérèse teach us is that there is a deep *okayness* to life despite all the contradictory evidence. The mystics do not turn away from the injustice, cruelty and suffering in the world. When Pope Francis visited the island of Lampedusa after the tragic loss of the refugees who had drowned off the coast of the island, he addressed a very powerful question to the world, *Who will weep for these people?* This is what Jesus talks about when he says that those who mourn, those who feel compassion for the suffering and move to help them, are in fact blessed and will indeed be comforted.

Mature spirituality has to grow through the brokenness that the prophets identified in our beautiful but flawed world. Those who live with the dark learn to see a new light, those who live in poverty of spirit are truly rich, those who weep feel a deeper joy. This is not superficial religion; it is the path that is no path. John of the Cross invited us to travel it. It begins when we realise that our life may not be about fulfilment but much more about desire. The mystics tell us that only love can pass this way.

3. Seeing with a Contemplative Heart

> Blessed are the pure in heart, for they will see God.
>
> *Matthew 5:8*

It is a mistake to judge the contemplative path as just another way of praying. It is much more than that. Some do use it for its introspective and therapeutic benefits, but it also has a prophetic and missionary thrust. A gathering of people praying in this way are contributing in hidden ways to the peace of the world. Our fragmented world has great need of this silent healing power.

The aim of silent prayer is to close down the continuous flow of mental chatter in our minds. Our monkey minds, as the Buddhists call them, can never be totally silenced but we can reduce the chatter by entering into a deep listening that puts us in touch with the ground of our being. This quiet non-conceptual listening is at the heart of the contemplative path. There are undoubted health benefits and there are those who use meditation for this purpose: it can reduce stress and lower blood pressure. But there is much more to it than that. Since the contemplative revival in the last century, scientists have had around fifty years of experience to study and the most fascinating finding is that contemplative prayer *transforms and changes the way a person thinks.* It is not about content but about *how* you think. It rewires the brain and changes the way you see. It opens the neural pathways between the mind and the heart so that you can perceive the underlying unity of everything. This is non-dual consciousness, or unitive consciousness as it is sometimes described.

What was once attained only by the greatest saints and mystics is now happening to many people in our world. It is a crucial step in the evolution in human consciousness and it is happening in time to meet the new challenges of our globalised world. The attraction for Christians is that this is exactly how Jesus perceived reality. He called it *The Kingdom of God* and when he was asked where it could be found he said it cannot be seen externally, *It is within you.* Biblical scholars all agree that this kingdom consciousness was at the core of his teaching. He lived the connected life, he was one with God, *I and the Father are One,* one with the Other, *Whatever you do to the least of these you do to me,* and one with creation as he spent time in the hills at prayer. It is a way of seeing the world from the perspective of abundance, of generosity and of mercy. Our ordinary mindset struggles with this. Why?

You only need to try silent prayer for a few minutes to discover the endless chatter that goes on in our minds, the endless procession of thoughts that grab our attention. Our over-stimulated culture makes it even more difficult than in past ages. No matter how disciplined you try to become you cannot entirely stop this chatter. What you can do – and this is central to what is called *Centering Prayer* – is to learn how to let these thoughts go. As soon as you become aware of a distracting thought just let it go and return your loving attention to the God within you in the core of your being. By this method you transform thoughts from being enemies of prayer into opportunities for a profound act of love. Centering prayer suggests that you choose a word such as *God, Jesus, Spirit, love* or *peace* and use that as your sacred word to bring your attention back to God. You don't have to say the word externally, just say in your heart, and you can do this no matter what the distraction is. It is important not to get worried about the chattering mind. Our thoughts give us so many opportunities for the action of letting go. Don't try to push them away forcefully.

Be gentle with yourself. Centering prayer is not about success. The point of the practice is just to do it each day for about twenty minutes. It is a *win/win* situation. Even though we may be beset by endless chatter, the Holy Spirit is at work in our inner being. The fruits of this kind of prayer is experienced in the rewiring of how we see reality. How does this work?

A New Way of Seeing

In her book *Centering Prayer and Inner Awakening* Cynthia Bourgeault[8] uses an image from the age of computers. She describes how our normal everyday way of looking at reality and at people is with the binary mind. She calls this the egoic operating system. It is very useful for organising the world into manageable bits. As a binary system it divides things as *inside/outside, up/down, subject/object, them/us, believers/ non-believers* and so on. But, as mentioned earlier, it cannot deal with the fundamental issues such as mystery, birth, death, love, suffering and eternity.

The egoic operating system governs the way most of us see the world. We identify ourselves with what differentiates us from others. So I describe myself as a male, an Englishman, a Catholic, a priest, a Salesian, a lover of sport and the music of the blues and so on. If these differences remain primary, it is very difficult to experience unitive consciousness. If we are seeking oneness and the basic way we look at reality is through difference, we are caught in a trap. There appears to be no way out. But none of these differences is primary.

---

8. Cynthia Bourgeault, *Centering Prayer and Inner Awakening* (Cowley Publications 2004)

What is primary is the gift of being – what the mystics call, *I am* – which I have received from the Ground of all Being. This is something which I share with every single person on the planet, irrespective of race, gender and religion.

The way out, Bourgeault suggests, is that there is an upgrade available to all of us. We have to move to new software, a new operating system. We have to move beyond all the images we have of ourselves and others, beyond the cult of the descriptive self. This is a radical challenge in our capitalist culture which is strongly focussed on images. The scarcity model which dominates our capitalist culture urges us to accumulate as much as we can to feel good about ourselves. It hinges on constantly comparing ourselves favourably or unfavourably as the case may be with other people. If I am challenged or threatened my reptilian brain either goes on the attack or runs away.

My real self, however, is buried beneath all these particular differences which I use to present myself to the world. That is why Jesus asks what profit would we gain by accumulating wealth when we never get in touch with our souls. It is only when we get beyond having to protect and defend our description of ourselves that we become truly free. If all I have is the particular descriptions of myself, I will put all my energy into defending myself in the face of any other person who will threaten me. I will certainly not be able to love my enemies as Jesus tells me to do.

The new software is learning how to see with the heart. For the mystics the heart represents the core of our being not our emotional centre. This is a contemplative way of seeing. Such awareness reveals that we are not limited by a particular self-image, but as a child of God I can simply see that *I am*. My feeling good about myself doesn't come from the responses, reactions and contrasts with others. It is rooted in the Being of God who loves me unconditionally. The next step is to see the Other also as a child of God, and so it goes on and on until it reaches my enemy who now appears – and is in truth – my brother or sister.

We are freed from all the negative fears that have dominated our lives, all the false judgments that we have made, and we begin to look out at the world with the eyes of Jesus. This is not naïve romanticism, it is truthful realism. It doesn't mean that we may not like someone; it means that we don't allow that negative judgement to block the creative freedom of love from changing the relationship for the better.

When spiritual teachers say that you can never find your True Self with your ego this is what they are talking about. It is not because the ego is bad; the problem is located in the egoic operating system. A world view based on scarcity is threatened by one based on abundance. It cannot perceive oneness. It cannot conceive a *me* that isn't differentiated from others by my unique qualities. It becomes anxious and fearful. We see this happening in the response of many rich nations to the plight of migrants desperate to escape war and violence. While most people operate out of an egocentric world view, nations operate at an ethnocentric consciousness. They are dominated by fear of the foreigner, the stranger, the immigrant, the ones who are identified as *them* and not *us*. This is at the heart of the crises we are experiencing today. We need to make the necessary shift from an ethnocentric to a world centric way of seeing. It is not a pious sentiment but an increasing necessity for the safety of everybody. We have weapons of great destructive power but we are still living at a low level of consciousness.

The Axial Age

I doubt whether everyone will attain this level of consciousness, but we do need a critical mass that can shift the way we connect with others. Karl Jaspers[9] identified a period from around 800 to 200 BC when many of the great religions emerged. He called it *The Axial Age*. It witnessed the emergence of Hinduism, Buddhism, Confucianism, Daoism and Jewish monotheism, and, particularly in Greece, Philosophical Rationalism. Wisdom figures such as Buddha, Confucius, Lao Tzu, Jeremiah, Ezekiel and Socrates emerged. It was a time of violent societies who sacralised their violence in rituals being slowly transformed into gentler ways by religious leaders. At the heart of this transformation was a turning to compassion.

Many contemporary observers are suggesting that if we are to survive our current crises we need to move into a second Axial Age. In recent centuries we have suffered a very unhealthy division between science and technology on the one hand, and religion on the other. Today many scientists are teaching religious believers to be more humble in their attitude to truth. Mature religion can teach science and secularism that we are not isolated individuals fighting each other for scarce resources. At the highest level of consciousness we are all united. This is not just a pious hope; it is a philosophical truth, but it does require moving beyond the limits of the mind and learning to see in a new way. This new way doesn't ignore the mind but places it inside a deeper place of seeing, what spiritual teachers call the heart.

It would be a mistake to understand this as a shift to emotion and sentimentality. It is much deeper than that: it denotes the heart as an organ of perception. This skill lies latent in all

---

9. *The Origin and Goal of History* (Routledge 2011)

of us but it seems to take some years to emerge. It is what a few enlightened people called mystics have known and experienced for centuries, but it is increasingly emerging in our contemporary world, though many religious believers and teachers are still unaware of it. The key to this way of seeing is that it perceives from the whole; it is a holographic perception and it avoids breaking everything into small bits and pieces. It's a bit like looking at a stained glass window and seeing the image of a saint rather than a set of coloured pieces. It is a vital stage in our search for spiritual maturity: it allows us to connect the dots and see the unity in all things.

In her seminal work on the Axial Age,[10] Karen Armstrong underlines two very important lessons provided by the wise men who led this period of spiritual transformation. The first is the necessity of self-critical thinking on the spiritual path. Instead of criticising others, healthy religion challenges us to criticise ourselves. This was the task of the great Jewish prophets such as Jeremiah, Amos, Hosea and Ezekiel. When Israel was threatened by powerful neighbours the tendency was to proclaim Yahweh as their God who would enable them to defeat their enemies. The prophets, on the contrary, warned the people to examine their own conduct instead of vilifying their enemies. Even during their painful exile in Babylon, Ezekiel advised them to focus on their own failures. Jesus took up the same position when he warned us against trying to take the splinter out of our brother's eye while neglecting the plank in our own.

As we look at the problems of our world today the answer remains the same. If we wish to change the world for the better, we have first to change ourselves and reform our own religion.

---

10. Karen Armstrong, *The Great Turnaround* (Atlantic Books, London 2006)

Fortunately we have wise leaders such as the Dalai Lama, Rabbi Jonathan Sacks and Pope Francis who are reminding us of this crucial aspect of mature religious belief. Sadly there are many believers who do not want to hear this message. Religion is then trapped at an immature level and changes nothing. The same pattern can be observed in the often vitriolic attacks of religion by aggressive atheists like Richard Dawkins. Bigotry is clearly not the answer.

The second lesson we can learn from the Axial Age is to promote compassion as the kernel of all mature religion. Religion is much more than doctrines and beliefs. They are important elements of religion but the wisest teachers of the Axial Age pointed to the transcendence of the Ultimate Reality that we call God. Ultimately God is Mystery, and no matter how good our theological ideas we will never fully grasp the Mystery. We can only approach this mystery with a profound humility. Too much certainty about our doctrines and beliefs quickly leads to the arrogance and superiority of feeling *we are right and they are wrong,* them and us.

A Mystical Vision

When we do attempt to approach the Great Mystery we find that we are already within it. It is not something outside us. This is the great insight shared by all the mystics. Some contemporary prophets are predicting that just as the last millennium was devoted to the theoretical exploration of cognition, the current millennium will be devoted to the theoretical exploration of love. I hope this prediction comes true, but I would add that we cannot restrict the exploration of love to the level of theory. Love has to be practised. Nor can we reduce love to a private activity between individuals. Mature love is expansive and reaches beyond the enjoyment of Eros to include the self-giving of agape. Moreover we will never understand human love unless we learn how to surrender to the deepest mystery that is Divine Love. This is where the mystics want to lead us. They invite us to move beyond acquaintance with God, even friendship with God, to the intimacy of union.

To live at a level of unitive consciousness or non-duality does not eliminate differences from our experience. Our world is full of difference, contradictions and dilemmas. But rather than get trapped into one side against the other, non-dual consciousness recognises the contradictions and paradoxes and holds them together at a deeper level. There is a shadow side to everything and any Catholic, for example, who refused to believe that about the Church has had to face the scandals of sexual abuse and the attempts by the hierarchy to cover them up.

What we are learning from our mystics is that only a contemplative mind can honour the underlying unity of all things while recognising and working with the differences. A contemplative seeing with the heart doesn't reject the mind; it places it within the heart. When heart, mind and body are correctly aligned we begin to see as Jesus saw. This is what Paul calls *putting on the mind of Christ.*

Such seeing will be at the heart of a new Axial Age. Shocked and horrified as we are with religious inspired violence and hatred of the Other, we can be greatly encouraged by the coming together of various Christian religions to pray and work together for a new world. Since the document *Nostra Aetate* of Vatican II, the Catholic Church has opened up to recognise and respect the wisdom traditions of the East. The first Axial Age responded to the shift from tribal consciousness to recognise the dignity of each individual. It was a necessary turn to the self.

Today in our electronically connected world our political and economic systems are struggling. Pope Francis has warned of the dangers of a purely market-driven economy and its effects on the poor. We need a new global consciousness. This is where mature religion can rise to the challenge. We need a new and deeper ecumenism: one that challenges each religion to get in touch with its own rich tradition and refashion it for a new age. For Christians, I think this is the recovery of the mystical path. Non-dual thinking teaches us that while there are many paths in the spiritual journey we are all moving towards the Infinite Love of the One God. The paradox here is that we are already totally immersed in the Great Mystery, the Great Love, the Great Compassion and the Great Mercy. This is the purpose of all religion. The challenge today is to awaken to this great truth.

4. Lights-On Mysticism

The light itself is one and all those who see it and love it are one.

St Augustine

When Pope Paul VI proclaimed Teresa of Ávila a Doctor of the Church in 1970, Karl Rahner commented that he was not just recognising the role of women in the Church but he was also affirming the gift of mysticism. It meant that those who teach mysticism are also teaching theology. Given the pace of change and the challenges of our times we need both our theologians and our mystics, and preferably theologians who are also mystics, as was normal in the first thousand years of Christianity. The mystics have been described as those who undertake the journey that the theologians write about. Whatever the case, they do have something unique to tell us about the unconditional and infinite mystery of God's love and what it means to respond to this love and live inside it.

One of the reasons why the Church may have lost touch with its mystical tradition is that mystical experience is described as ineffable, it cannot really be put into words. In the years of the Enlightenment, Church teachers sought to reduce the spiritual life to doctrines and dogmas. We chose the path of the rational mind alone. We forgot the wisdom of St Augustine who said, *Si comprehendis non est Deus: if you can grasp it it's not God.* Mysticism became a well-kept secret. Maybe this is because it doesn't sit well with state or Church power; it cannot be managed or controlled. The entrance into the mystical path is essentially one of humility and poverty; it is not something we can plan for or programme. Essentially it is a relational path that leads to vulnerability and intimacy. As Thomas Merton says it is not something we can grab hold of or grasp for ourselves; it can only be received.

Meister Eckhart says that the spiritual journey is about subtraction not addition. Rather than piling up spiritual experiences, it is much more about subtraction – letting go. This seems closer to the spiritual path taught by Jesus: he enjoyed people and the things of this world, but he did not cling to anything, even Godhead, as Paul tells us. Contemplative prayer is the best way to open ourselves to this grace and the clearing away of the obstacles of the False Self.

In *Guidelines to Mystical Prayer*,[11] Ruth Burrows makes a useful distinction between Lights-On mysticism and Lights-Off mysticism. She relates the contrasting experience of two friends of hers. One lived an active life and enjoyed a lively mystical life. The other, living in a contemplative order, had no such experiences despite many years of contemplative practice. Both reached transforming union. Sr Ruth describes her own lack of any felt experience of God in her life as a Carmelite nun. Like John of the Cross, she teaches that pure faith and pure love are the essence of contemplative prayer. We have no faculty of the soul that can perceive this. The Holy Spirit is often at work in our souls and we have little or no awareness. Thomas Keating maintains that around five per cent of the contemplatives he knows enjoy Lights-On mysticism. According to him they are all either married or engaged in active ministry. The point of prayer is daily fidelity to the practice. Before looking at Lights-Off mysticism in the next chapter it will be helpful to look at some Lights-On happenings which have been recorded.

Moses

One of the earliest recorded mystical events in the Jewish scriptures is the experience of Moses and the burning bush

---

11. Continuum (2007)

in chapter three of Exodus. It is important to recall that Moses was no candidate for sanctity when this occurred. He was on the run in a foreign country having killed one of its inhabitants. He was a man living on the edge and had just led his flock beyond the wilderness close to Mount Horeb, the mountain associated with God, when he sees the burning bush. He hears God's voice calling him by name, but is told, *Come no nearer* and he must take off his shoes because he is standing on holy ground.

Here we find fascinating details of a *God/human* encounter. The transcendent, formless mystery that we call God begins a conversation with a mere mortal. Infinite Divinity seeks a relationship with a finite and flawed human being. There is an invitation, an allurement, a fascination at the heart of this encounter, and the flames of the bush offer warmth and light. God doesn't threaten Moses with annihilation he asks him to stand his ground. God establishes a secure framework for intimacy. There is nothing to fear; Moses will not be swallowed up and lose his identity. Some level of equality is necessary in a healthy relationship and God is inviting Moses into a relationship of mutuality, of give-and-take. Love is not absorption, the love of God is a flame that burns but does not destroy. Difference is not an obstacle to this level of intimacy. God accepts us as we are, the good and the bad.

The whole event says something very profound about our identity. We are not isolated individuals. We are all unique but we grow and mature our personhood in and through relationships. We are made for relationship and for connection, not isolation and separation. If mystics are those whose lives are so transformed that they are one with God, one with everyone else and one with creation, we can see all aspects of this truth revealed in this encounter. God invites Moses into the relationship, then he gives him a task.

A mystical encounter is not just a private little event, it always has ramifications for how we relate to others. So God tells Moses that he has heard the cry of his people suffering as slaves in Egypt and he commissions him to be his instrument in freeing the people. The inward journey of mystical encounter between human and divine is always an opening to create a more just and better world. Mysticism and Justice are two sides of the same coin. We need both an inward and an outward journey for true human flourishing. Finally in this encounter we see the connection of the spiritual journey to nature, to the whole of creation. God appears not in a temple but in a burning bush. In instructing Moses to take off his shoes, God is teaching him about the holiness of creation.

Saul/Paul

We have another unlikely candidate for holiness. Saul, a man who approved of the killing of Stephen, is actively engaged in eliminating the followers of Jesus, when on the road to Damascus he has a mystical vision in which he is struck to the ground. This is a humbling experience for this law-abiding Pharisee, and he is astonished when he hears the voice of God identifying with the very people he is trying to root out and destroy. Moreover he is blinded, a powerful symbol of how an encounter with God changes the way we see reality.

Later, in chapter twelve of his second letter to the Corinthians, Paul relates another profound mystical experience:

> I know a person in Christ who fourteen years ago was caught up to the third heaven – whether in the body or out of the body I do not know; God knows. And I know that such a person – whether in the body or out of the body I do not know; God knows – was caught up into Paradise and heard things that are not to be told, that no mortal is permitted to repeat.[12]

---
12. 2 Corinthians 12:2-4

Now he is speaking from his True Self and he uses the expression which more than any other describes the result of the transformative path, *in Christ*. This is Paul's favourite and oft-quoted phrase to describe his own transformation. In relating his mystical experience he demonstrates the reticence of the true mystic who cannot and should not put his experience into words. Here we have the ineffability of the mystical encounter. In the next paragraph of his letter he goes to the heart of the essential virtue of the mystical life: humility. He is aware that his revelatory experience is exceptional, even dangerous, and so he adds some of the most extraordinary words in all the scriptures.

> To keep me from being too elated, a thorn was given to me in the flesh, a messenger of Satan to torment me, to keep me from being too elated. Three times I appealed to the Lord about this, that it would leave me, but he said to me, *My grace is sufficient for you, for power is made perfect in weakness.*[13]

A mystical vision can never be claimed as a personal achievement. This is a defeat for the ego and we all suffer from a religious ego, which likes to pile up our virtues and *holy* experiences to make ourselves worthy in the eyes of God. All spiritual teachers place humility at the heart of the spiritual path. It is not about achieving worthiness – an impossible task – but a much more challenging task: without some dying of the ego, or the *False Self* as it is called, transformation cannot happen. Even though Paul begged God to release him from his thorn in the flesh, God refuses to do so. What a lesson for all of us! Even a mystical vision as profound as Paul's could become a trap for the ego. Grace is a gift. We cannot control our relationship with Divine Mystery. We can only remain open, empty and poor and wait for God to invade us, when and where he will.

---

13. 2 Corinthians 12:7-9

Hildegard von Bingen[14]

Born in 1098 as the last of ten children, she was dedicated to God and at the age of eight was sent to live with a holy anchoress named Jutta, whose small house was attached to the Abbey of St Disibod in the Rhineland. Jutta helped to immerse the young Hildegard into the oceanic love of God that surrounds us at all times. Her growing awareness of the love and beauty of God was further developed through words, images and music. At the same time she was quite a stubborn young girl and a bit self-righteous. Although she experienced many visions as a young girl, the culture of those times discouraged her from communicating them. As she gained in years she became more aware of the dark side of life: corruption even in the Church; the laziness of priests and the neglect of creation.

She wanted to protest about what she was seeing around her but she was a woman in a very patriarchal world and Church. How could she possibly find a voice? Her spiritual director and her superiors were telling her that she had no authority to speak out, that her role was just to get on with her everyday duties. Aflame with the anger and fire of the prophets, but unable to give voice, she became ill.

The turning point occurred in the forty-third year of her life. She had a mystical vision of great radiance. A voice told her that, despite being a weak and frail woman, she had to speak out. She rose from her bed greatly emboldened and began to write her first book which she called *Knowing the Way*. Her visions gave her great confidence and the words poured out, as if from the power and energy of God flowing through her.

---

14. I am indebted to June Boyce-Tillman for much of this information in Chapter 12 of *Journey to the Heart*, (Canterbury Press 2011)

Thus began a whole new way of life as the great and the good of her time visited or corresponded with her, including the Pope and Bernard of Clairvaux.

Jutta's house was too small for Hildegard's fast growing community and she moved to a new foundation near Bingen. It was spacious and comfortable, and included piped water because Hildegard's love of the Creator God could not envisage him wanting anyone to live in discomfort. It was a life dedicated to God through poetry, music and drama, including books about women's issues, medicine and natural history, theology and the lives of the saints. She was invited to visit the great cathedrals of Germany and denounced corruption from the pulpit.

In October 2012 Hildegard was declared a Doctor of the Church by Pope Benedict XVI. Like many of the mystics her message has been recovered for our times. One of her great mystical gifts is her deep awareness of the interconnectedness and interdependence of all things. For her, things are *penetrated* with connectedness and that penetration flows from the Holy Spirit. She describes the Spirit as the *fiery life* that infuses all things and radiates in and through everything. All things are ordered into a wholeness that is the wisdom of God, the Holy Spirit, and like many of the mystics she uses paradox to make connections between the contradictions of our experience. The spiritual journey challenges all of us not to deny the dark side of our lives. The good news at the heart of the Christian story is that God uses all of our experience and integrates it as we grow in consciousness. Nothing is wasted. God is the Great Recycler. The word *viriditas,* or *greenness* as we would say today, is at the heart of Hildegard's spirituality. Much more than simply a colour it represented fertility, health and vigour, and she saw it as God's love energising everything that exists.

This radiant love is present in all creation. This is not pantheism. Creation is not God, but without God's viriditas nothing would exist. While much of her medical advice would not be acceptable today, her main stress that we need to live balanced lives remains very relevant.

In our present time this message is more needed than ever and there are growing voices in our culture reminding us of our need to protect and care for the earth as well as caring for ourselves. We have a political group called the Green Party in European politics, which is attracting both young and old. It is good that people get angry with many of the injustices and evils of our time. At times, however, this anger appears as a kind of righteousness that divides the world into good and bad, those who are right and those who are wrong. This is where we need the wisdom of contemplation and non-dualism that can include all sides in the struggle to create a better world. Without this, many of the protest movements of our time seem to degenerate into violence. The American civil rights movement of the 1960s was led by Martin Luther King, himself a mystic. He chose the difficult path of non-violence. In contrast the civil rights movement of Northern Ireland's Catholics moved quickly from non-violence to violence, resulting in many needless deaths and great suffering on both sides. Today in the Arab world we are witnessing the idealism of the Arab Spring degenerating into violence resulting in thousands of deaths and millions of refugees, many of them children. As the tide of refugees begins to reach Europe, political leaders struggle to know how to react. We seem happy to encourage the globalisation of business; we don't know how to react to the globalisation of people.

Thomas Aquinas

The Dominican priest Thomas Aquinas was one of the most brilliant theological minds in Western Christianity. On the morning of December 6th 1273 he was celebrating Mass on the feast of St Nicholas. This was no ordinary morning for Thomas, who experienced a mystical vision during the Mass. We have no details of what really happened but on his return to his room where he had been working on his great work, the *Summa Theologica*, he dismissed his secretary, Fr Reginald, and wrote no more. He is reported to have said that in comparison with what he had just experienced everything he had written was just like straw.

This is a remarkable comment coming from a man universally regarded as one of the greatest theologians and philosophers in the history of the Church. What happened during that Mass we shall never know, but it underlines the remark Thomas once made – and echoed by another great theologian, St John of the Cross – that we cannot get to God with our minds but only through love. His *Summa Theologica* was never finished and Thomas died a few months later. Having glimpsed the ineffable Holy Mystery that is God, he was reduced to silence. Mysticism, whether Lights-On or Lights-Off, inevitably leads us to silence.

Thomas Merton

In this chapter I have concentrated on mystics who experienced visions, even ecstasies. Many others could have been mentioned such as Teresa of Ávila and John of the Cross. In the last century we had the figure of Thomas Merton who is credited as having been one of the most important influences in the recovery of the contemplative path for our times.

His own Lights-On vision occurred not inside his Cistercian monastery but outside on a street corner of Louisville, Kentucky on a Saturday afternoon in 1958 when he saw the beauty and radiance of the souls of ordinary people walking the streets while they were quite unaware of the light and brilliance at the core of their being. Years later, in *Conjectures of a Guilty Bystander,* he struggled to find words to express this ineffable experience, describing what he *saw* as a point of nothingness, a point of pure truth, a spark that belongs entirely to God, the person each one is in God's eyes. Reflecting on this vision, he concluded that if only we could see each other in this way there would be no more hatred, cruelty or war.

5. Lights-Off Mysticism

> Ask, and it will be given to you; search, and you will find; knock, and the door will be opened for you.
>
> *Matthew 7:7*

In our times the Holy Spirit seems to be inviting more people than ever before into an experience of non-dual mysticism. They may not have the visions of Lights-On mystics but their experiences of a direct encounter with Divine Reality are just as precious and life-changing and it appears to be the most common path, the path of Lights-Off Mysticism.

In January 2013 the oldest man in Britain died. His name was Reg Dean. He was an Anglican clergyman. On his 109th birthday he was interviewed on BBC North West News. Asked if he had any wisdom to impart, after so many years, he replied that all we have to do in life is to answer three questions:

>Who am I?
>Why am I here?
>Where am I going?

In our secular disenchanted world the answers still fascinate even though they often elude us. The contemporary search is too often diverted down the path of image and appearance. This is the path of the False Self that seeks security, approval of others, and control over our lives. It is the path of acquisition and competition and it fits neatly into our capitalist economy. It is the world of scarcity in which the strong and the powerful win and the poor and the weak lose. The task of all healthy religion, on the contrary, is to enable us to die to this False Self and awaken to our True Self, who we are in God, to answer Reg Dean's first question.

The problem with the False Self is not that it is bad or sinful. There are plenty of people who live morally good lives who are quite unaware of who they really are. They think that they are enjoying life to the full, especially if they have money and a comfortable life. Our materialist culture is happy to keep delivering the goods of greater and greater affluence. We have made a god of the *market* and even though this system experienced a major collapse in the credit crunch, governments, with greater or lesser success, have been trying to get back to those heady days of economic growth. As always, the poor are the ones who are bearing the most severe burdens. This is the world of scarcity when the rich seem to get richer and the poor poorer. Such a worldview inevitably leads to conflict and even war, as we see in many parts of our world today.

We need a new consciousness to help us make the transition from our individual, separate identity that cuts us off from the pain of the world to a new way of seeing and a new way of being. This is the whole point of religion: to show us how to re-connect with our original and True Self before we separated ourselves from the Holy Mystery that we call God. I don't think we can be too critical of the secular world for this. It was a necessary stage of growth from tribal consciousness to a separate sense of self as an individual. However it doesn't take us far in the spiritual journey. Immature religion doesn't help either. There is a religious False Self which appears when we identify too much with our virtues and our roles, in the search for liturgical correctness, and when we judge others harshly. Pope Francis is strongly aware of this in his attempts to reform the Church.

This reform has to be at the heart of new evangelisation. Without its mystical dimension, religion often appears as a moralistic game in which we are all doomed to failure. This is the first half of life done badly: religion reduced to moral rules, correctness and requirements. The False Self is too small and too private to surrender to the process of dying into a new life, what Christians call Christ consciousness. Transformation is at the goal of the spiritual journey. Mature religion reminds us that the gift is already given. It is not a case of having to earn or achieve our True Self, it is all about awakening to its mysterious and wondrous presence within. As Thomas Merton says, *What we have to become is who we already are.* Such a paradox confounds our dualistic minds.

What keeps the False Self in control is the ego. Jesus is clear in teaching that this has to die if we are to enjoy the fullness of life. He is speaking about the selfish ego. We all need an ego to live a well-adjusted life, but living inside our ego boundaries prevents us from growing into a new consciousness. Augustine called this *original sin*. Spiritual teachers today are more inclined to name it as the *human condition*. Thomas Keating identifies this as coming to reflexive self-consciousness without an awareness of the divine presence within. But the gift is there and it is celebrated by baptism, which blesses the presence of the Indwelling Trinity in our deepest being. The signing with the cross, the anointings, the pouring of water, are all aimed at revealing our true identity as sons or daughters of God. Spirituality is the deepening of this transformative awareness now in this world, not an insurance scheme for getting into heaven. It is not the pursuit of perfection by our effort and willpower, but a gracious receiving of the gift. This is the source of the peace and joy that passes all understanding. What we are searching for is already given. Why is it that we are not more aware of this? The ego/self is what keeps us from this awareness. The ego, as our protector in the early years of life, is rooted in fear. Unhealthy religion tends to keep many at that level. Their religious outlook is controlled by fear.

They cling to certainties and dismiss those who are different. There is no real spiritual journey because they already have the answers to every question. Others get distracted by the myriad ways of entertaining ourselves in this extraverted culture. It is the bread and circuses of our times and it includes the majority of people today. Again there is nothing wrong with entertainment; it is an enjoyable feature of life: it becomes a problem when it distracts us to the point of addiction and the complete neglect of any inner journey. For some it is the distraction of a workaholic life-style that keeps us from the journey within.

Why are we here?

Reg Dean's second question was, *Why am I here?* I would suggest that, if we have discovered our true identity as sons and daughters of God, we have a sure foundation for the journey within. Our purpose is an utterly extraordinary one: as imperfect and fallible human beings, we are all called to intimacy with Ultimate Reality, the Divine Mystery that we call God. This is the mystical path, the way of contemplation or more simply the way of prayer. Infinite Love has created our hearts in such a way that only Infinite Love will suffice. This is our DNA, and it is why we have been placed on this earth, not to win a race to get to heaven, but to enjoy divine union here and now. This is what Jesus is speaking about when he talks about the Kingdom of God. You don't have to look outside, says Jesus, *It is within you*. Ask and you will receive more because you already have the gift within. This is the world of abundance, the world of grace.

First-half-of-life religion keeps God at a distance. We are happy to worship God on a Sunday and even to work for him, as long as we can remain in control with our ego. The religious False Self likes to have commandments, moral rules and Church regulations to follow. We can feel good about ourselves as we measure our success in carrying out our religious duties. We forget that God has created plenty of worker ants to watch and delight in as aspects of his creation. What God wants from human beings is a relationship, one that grows from fear, through acquaintance, to friendship and intimacy into union. Our ego will resist this as we struggle between the desire of our soul and the fears of our False Self. Contemplative prayer is one way of beginning this journey but it is not an easy path. As we move from kataphatic to apophatic prayer, we are invited to surrender to the mystery of unknowing rather than knowing, where our finite love meets the Infinite Love of God. Even those who experience Lights-On mysticism also have to travel this path before they reach transforming union. John of the Cross makes the point that all the heavenly visions of Lights-On mysticism are not worth as much as the least act of humility.

Strictly speaking, centering prayer is not contemplative prayer; it is a practice that frees us up to receive the gift of grace that is contemplation. It emerges from and is rooted in the desire that God has planted in our souls. It would be wrong to see it as merely private prayer that cuts us off from others. As we sit in silent prayer we are connecting with the divine presence within. At the same time we also are connecting with the divine presence in everyone else, and with the divine presence in creation. We never initiate prayer; we join the mutual flow of divine love between Father, Son and Holy Spirit and this deepens with every practice. We are not in control here. It may take time, and we may think nothing is happening, but our identity is being revealed in the pattern of Jesus who shows us how to put the human and divine together. We may not have any felt experience of this but it continues at God's pace within us. Some days when we have endless distractions, the Holy Spirit may be deeply active in our unconscious. All we have to do is to bring our attention back to God with our sacred word.

The journey to intimacy is often a painful one. When we enter our inner world we become aware of all the fears that block our path to union with God. We face our own weaknesses and contradictions. We have to learn not to deny these but to embrace them and learn to forgive them, perhaps even weep over them.

The only way to heal the wounds of childhood is the way of the cross. Our broken human condition is where we experience the cross and there is no way of healing ourselves other than accepting this woundedness. This is what Paul learned directly from his own mystical vision. For most of us this path is a dark and mysterious one. All our limitations, all the hurts that we have suffered, all the ways we have felt the pain of the human condition, and all the ways we judge others are caught up in our experience of the way of the cross.

Here we encounter the heart of the Christian mystery, the pattern of death and life, of cross and resurrection. To go down into our brokenness is to encounter a different kind of darkness. St John of the Cross calls it *luminous darkness*. But the deeper our descent the closer we become to the Infinite Love of God who sees us as precious in our brokenness. We meet the divine paradox that the last shall be first. To take the lowest place is to sit in the highest place in the non-dual teaching of Jesus. When we encounter suffering that we cannot fix, we often turn to God to fix it for us; to take the pain and the weakness away. Mysticism reveals a God who is not an all-conquering, all-powerful figure but in fact a humble God who offers to carry our woundedness with us. This is how the infinite goodness of God is revealed to us. We are fully accepted as we are and so we can surrender our wounded selves, even our sins, to the infinite mercy of God. There is a part of each one of us that has always loved God. There is a part of us that is Love itself and that is what we fall into when we awaken to this wondrous mystery at the core of our being. We have been put on this earth to discover this loving mystery that is at the heart of everything. It's our true identity and all we have to do is to draw from that deep inner level of acceptance and abundance.

The great gift of contemplative prayer is that by owning our own failings we meet not judgement but compassion. As the False Self of success and achievement passes away, we are being opened up and prepared to embrace the woundedness of the world. To experience The Paschal Mystery of Jesus is to know the Father as Jesus knows the Father. We are being prepared for intimacy. Mystics such as Julian of Norwich know this from their own experience:

> If there be any lover of God on earth who is continually kept from falling, I do not know of it for it was not shown to me. But this was shown: that in falling and rising we are always tenderly protected in one love; for as God beholds us we do not fall, and as we behold ourselves we do not stand, and both of these seem to me to be true, but our Lord God's view is the highest truth.[15]

Here is the paradox at the heart of the spiritual path. The spiritual journey is not about achieving perfection. Mature spirituality is always a both/and experience. Trained in our dualistic minds we find it difficult to understand this paradox. What the mystics teach is sometimes called the *third eye*. This might seem a strange concept but as you read these words you are using both your eyes, which from their different angles produce one image in the brain.

---

15. Julian of Norwich, *Revelations of Divine Love* (translated by Elisabeth Spearing, Penguin Classics 1998) p.175-6

Your brain offers you two different angles and the reconciliation of difference. It's normal; we do it every day. Yes, we are both sinners and saints, we are dark and light, but as we own these opposites we discover a reconciling third which is in fact the Holy Spirit. That is why Julian tells us with confidence that while in our finite reality we are both sinners and saints, at a deeper level the infinite reality of God enfolds us in merciful and forgiving love. We may not be perfect, but we are holy. Paul emphasises this paradox in chapter eight of his letter to the Romans:

> If God himself has taken up residence in your life, you can hardly be thinking more of yourself than him. Anyone, of course, who has not welcomed this invisible but clearly present God, The Spirit of Christ, won't know what we are talking about. But for you who welcome him – in whom he dwells – even though you still experience all the limitations of sin – you yourself experience life on God's terms.[16]

The anonymous writer of *The Cloud of Unknowing* makes the same point in drawing a distinction between two kinds of humility, one imperfect and the other perfect. The first is based on our weakness, frailty and sinfulness, and the fact that however we might progress in virtue this sinful dimension remains. The second is based on moving from our brokenness to the thought of God's goodness and mercy. It can happen that a soul may be granted such a sense of union with the Divine that he forgets any awareness of his own being, his holiness or his sinfulness. Such a grace is usually fleeting and there is no possibility of experiencing it without first experiencing imperfect humility.

---

16. *The Message* Translation op cit

Consciousness

When John of the Cross describes mysticism as luminous darkness he is trying to combine the subtle changes and transformations that contemplative prayer offers us. All we have to do is to enter the silence and the darkness beyond our everyday senses to awaken our spiritual senses. With regularity of practice we begin to see in the dark. We all know what it is like to walk from bright sunlight into a darkened room. It takes time for our eyes to adjust.

This is very counter-intuitive for the Western mind that we have all inherited. We think we are fully conscious when our brains are engaged in thinking. This is the binary mind that seeks to compare, contrast, divide and judge reality. As we grow in spiritual consciousness we discover a different way of seeing and a different way of knowing. It is a *knowing with* rather than a *knowing about*. Mature consciousness is a falling into a much more spacious place, something much bigger than the private, separate self. The False Self cannot do this. It involves connecting into a larger mystery, a larger truth, a larger love, a larger life. This is the door to the suffering and joys of the world. This is the way the mystics see reality. Most Christians have been brought up to consider this kind of seeing as reserved for the few. In fact, it is central to Christianity and it is clearly how Jesus saw the world, from the perspective of what he called *The Kingdom of God*.

We have been taught that salvation is a private programme for getting us into heaven and we have lost sight of the fact that salvation involves a transformation of consciousness for life in this world. This is why Jesus became human: to teach us how to put the divine and the human, the spiritual and the material together. Mysticism is not a private affair; it connects us at the deepest intimacy with God, others, and creation.

At this level of connection our private sins are much easier to carry and own. In the Jewish scriptures we see Yahweh wooing Israel as a people, as a collective. Non-dual seeing is not just about *me* as the False Self would have it. This level of communion makes it possible for us, on the one hand, to carry the burden of shame for our brokenness and at the same time to bear *the weight of glory,* as Paul calls it. Mysticism, therefore, lets us know that we don't have to take ourselves too seriously. A sure sign of the False Self is an unwillingness to let others tease us. A sense of humour that allows us to laugh at ourselves is a much underrated aspect of the spiritual journey.

One of the most disturbing aspects of present times is the increase in the suicide rate particularly among young people. Now that the cosmic egg of meaning provided by religion has been replaced by a purely secular outlook, it leaves them very exposed, having to carry the burden of living an isolated individual life while living in a disenchanted world. Intimacy becomes very difficult when it gets reduced to genital sexual activity, as all too frequently happens. It is not entirely their fault. Today neuroscience is confirming the importance of the times when a mother gazes with love into the eyes of her baby. At those special times mirror neurons are formed. When this happens we have the security and the ability to move from fear to love. Tenderness, closeness, intimacy then becomes much easier. It is very difficult to open ourselves to an intimate relationship with Infinite Love if we haven't experienced finite love. Without such experience we cannot move into the spaciousness of the world of grace, mercy and forgiveness that makes true intimacy possible. Recently I met a young Pakistani asylum seeker whose hand was slashed by a knife as she was trying to protect her face from the hatred of a total stranger. For a young man to attack a young woman in such an unprovoked way indicates deep wounding.

All mature religions teach the importance of how to look at the world. It is not just what we do that matters it is how we see. At the higher levels of consciousness our seeing is transformed. We learn to see God in everything. Our individual eyes with their inevitably narrow point of view are transformed into universal eyes. We can now begin to look beyond those we love, like and approve, to look at everyone and everything with love and reverence. We are able to re-enchant the world.

6. Beyond yet Intimate

> Everything you are and think and do is permeated with Oneness.
> *Paul's Letter to the Ephesians 4:6*[17]

> Let us make humankind in our image, according to our likeness.
> *Genesis 1:26*

To walk the spiritual journey is to encounter paradox. The language also can confuse us: the idea of dying to our False Self; the talk of surrender; giving away; and phrases such as *the dark night of the soul*. We learn that all these apparent negatives are leading us into the most rich and wonderful fullness of our lives. We learn that the dark side of our lives is the place where the transforming light of God enters. We learn that our sins don't drive us away from God; they draw him closer to us in compassionate love. Even when we experience the raw pain of suffering and loss, we reach a deeper place where his presence is found. If we can overcome the fear of giving up our own point of view as the only means of reading reality, we fall into the great spaciousness of love and acceptance, which draws us beyond a world of scarcity into a world of abundance. And so it goes on. But the greatest paradox of all is the discovery that the Transcendent Being, the Creator of everything that exists, wants to have an intimate relationship with each one of us, his creatures. The Infinite Love, that is God, appears to be drawn to the limitations of our finite humanity. When God looks at us he sees that we are precious in our brokenness, and he cannot resist that. Our longing for God is indeed God's longing for us.

---

17. *The Message* Translation op cit

The Beyond

As we are emerging from the limitations of the Enlightenment some of our scientists are helping us to move to a deeper level of engagement with the mystery of God. To say that God is transcendent is to recognise that God is beyond our understanding and comprehension. Because of the quantum revolution, scientists have moved away from the claims of the past that we could achieve objective certainty about the world in which we live. Today many take a much humbler position. As we have tried to probe the mysteries of the universe in which we find ourselves, it appears that we know very little about it. Neil Turok, one of the world's leading theoretical physicists, claims that our attempts to understand the universe have created a set of incredibly complicated models that often contradict each other. We are in the territory of unknowing rather than knowing. This is mystical language.

This might trouble those who taught the catechisms of recent years as they tried to answer every possible question about Christian faith, even suggesting we could define, set limits on, God. But it wouldn't have troubled great minds such as The Cappodocian Fathers in the East, nor figures like Augustine, Denys the Areopagite, Meister Eckhart and others in the West. They realised that our minds cannot make sense of the God that we call Trinity because it calls us to a deeper level of consciousness, beyond our rational minds. While the rational mind is locked into logic and duality in the way it perceives reality, the non-dual mind is able to live inside the mystery of the paradox that God is both One and Three at the same time. Today, where some scientists confidently dismiss belief in God as irrational because of lack of proof, others would be open to the presence of mystery at the heart of reality. They are more likely to be saying that statements about God are beyond their competence.

Even our theologians are placing themselves in the camp of those who say that our language about God is much more in the realm of symbol and metaphor. We are all, it seems, in the Cloud of Unknowing in the face of the Transcendence of God. Even though our scientists are telling us that the universe is much stranger than we thought, what they do seem to agree on is the inter-connectedness that holds everything together. Theologians such as Karl Rahner and Bernard Lonergan have highlighted the mystical dimension of how we connect with the Transcendent Mystery we call God. It is a mystery of participation. We do not gaze at God as if he were an object. The mystery of the Trinity cannot be grasped by our thinking minds; it has to be participated in. It involves a practical response on our behalf. The deepest truth is the unconditional love of God, and we are all, in our very physical bodies, manifestations of the love of God. The contemplative life is a process of awakening to that fact and we find our deepest joy by participating in the mystery.

Our Christian faith reveals and teaches that God has placed this hunger within us. In the striking words of the mystic Catherine of Genoa, *My deepest me is God.* This Divine Mystery hidden and beyond our understanding is at the same time a relational mystery of knowledge and love. The first manifestation of God is intimacy and the purpose of our life is to discover ourselves not outside but inside this mystery of love that we call God. *The Beyond* that is God is closer than we could ever imagine.

A Relational Mystery

From all eternity, God as origin and creator has been eternally expressing himself as *The Word*. Our poetical language calls him *Father*, although if we lived in a matriarchal society we would call him *Mother*, because he includes all gender.

In article 239 of the Catechism of the Catholic Church we read:
> God transcends the human distinction between the sexes. He is neither man nor woman: he is God.[18]

God as Word is the *logos* who knows the Father intimately as God. The Father in saying himself as the Word contemplates himself as the Word, and the Son contemplates the Father. The intimate life of God is a contemplative life. This infinite communion of intimacy gives rise to an Infinite Love and that Infinite Love is the Holy Spirit. The divine relations within the Trinity are all about the giving and receiving of love.

How can we speak of God as personal? When the apostles ask Jesus if they can see the Father, Jesus says, *He who sees me sees the Father.* We cannot see God as Father as a separate private individual. The Trinity is not made up of three separate individuals. The same is true with regard to the Christ as the Eternal Word of God. There is no separate Christ. He is one with the Father, as he tells us in John's gospel. The same is true of the Holy Spirit, because the Holy Spirit is the Infinite Love that arises from the Infinite Love between the Father and the Son. These three persons are continuously giving themselves to each other in distinction, yet at the same time in union in the fullness of love. The life of God is a transpersonal life of infinite communion rooted in intimacy. This is not easy for us to understand. It is like reading poetry. We have to sit and ponder.

When God the Father contemplates himself in the Son from all eternity he also contemplates the existence of all things in creation. This is true of all created things.

---

18. *Catechism of the Catholic Church* art. 239

As we read in John's prologue:
> In the beginning was the Word, and the Word was with God, and the Word was God. All things came into being through him, and without him not one thing came into being. What has come to being in him was life and the life was the light of all people.[19]

Everything created reflects the presence of God; it is God's body and we can contemplate God in the concrete reality of all things. For Julian of Norwich it was a hazelnut; for Francis of Sales it was a rose. This is not pantheism, for without God's enlivening Spirit none of these things – including ourselves – would continue to exist.

In *New Seeds of Contemplation,* Thomas Merton describes how we participate in this cosmic dance of God in creation:
> When we are alone on a starlit night, when by chance we see the migrating birds in autumn descending on a grove of junipers to rest and eat; when we see children in a moment when they are really children, when we know love in our own hearts.[20]

We can all think of moments like this when the veil grows thin and we get a sense of God's presence. It may be special moments when we are alone looking at the ocean, or walking in the hills, sharing with a friend, or it can be everyday happenings when we see the face of a beggar, or a mother holding the hand of her child, or boys caught up in the thrill of a game, or girls sharing laughter and friendship. When we develop a regular contemplative practice these moments happen more readily. Our way of seeing is changed as we perceive the unity in all things and catch a glimpse of God playing, as Merton says, *in the garden of his creation.*

---

19. Jn 1:1-4
20. Thomas Merton, *New Seeds of Contemplation* (New Directions, 1961)

This is the daily miracle that Infinite Love is being manifest in the finiteness of creation. It is nothing less than the Invisible Uncreated Love that is God being made manifest in the concrete reality of our lives.

We tend to think of our lives as beginning in the womb of our mother, but in reality we have always existed in the eternal love of God. The letter to the Ephesians begins by telling us that before the world was made God chose us in Christ. This is why Paul describes our lives as hidden with Christ in God. This is the *you* that was never born and the *you* that will never die. This is what it means to be a person. Our essence is rooted in an infinite relationship, and we participate as persons in the infinite relations of the Trinity. We exist as persons as manifestations of the Infinite, and we are given a human nature so that we can become increasingly conscious of ourselves, of others and all things, as touched by the divine. If we go back to the question asked by Reg Dean – *Why am I here?* – we can say, *It is to recognise that the gift of life is the generosity of God.* Our human nature is given to us so that we can recognise the sacredness and the beauty of all life. And we are given the gift of freedom to say *Yes* to who we eternally are.

This freedom is real because love can never be imposed, imposed love is not love. The freedom is also real in that we can say *No* to who we are in God as we try to live our lives separate from who we really are. This is the root of our unhappiness, yet we find it so difficult to give up our separateness. God's answer to this is revealed in the second person of the Trinity taking on our human nature. He becomes one of us, carries the burden of our separateness and our limitations. He shares our problems, is drawn into the tragic nature of our human condition. On every page of the gospel story God reveals that we are precious to him in our brokenness.

God's love for us is not dependent on what we do or say. That is why Merton describes our True Self as not being subject to the brutalities of our own will or the actions of anyone else. No matter what anyone does to you there is something in you that cannot be touched; it is invincible because it is the gift and mark of Infinite Love.

God's Longing

God is always the initiator in the spiritual journey. When we awaken to the longing for God in the deepest part of our being, we are responding to the longing God has for us. The movement of total giving and receiving of love between the three persons of the Trinity includes all of us. We are created for this divine union and it is offered to every single person on the planet, saint and sinner. God is always inviting us to participate in the circle of contemplative gazing. Julian of Norwich teaches that we will experience the fullness of joy when we learn how to behold God in everything. Beholding or gazing is central to any contemplative practice.

There is a moment when a mother gazes into the eyes of her child and the child gazes back in the safety of unconditional love. I remember one morning sitting on a bus returning home after having left a car in the garage for servicing. I was the only male on the bus. After a while a young mother got on the bus with a young child and sat on the front seat. The child turned round to look at and connect with all of us on the bus by smiling and waving. All the women were charmed and responded to the innocence of the baby. Even I, as I sat at the back of the bus as a male cleric reading the Book of Leviticus, had to smile and connect with this child. The Church tells us that the child has this Eden-like innocence and openness to connection until the age of seven. That is when the rational binary mind takes over and the sense of union is lost.

This has to happen as we develop our separate individuality but we spend the rest of our lives trying to get back to Eden. As we saw earlier, the secret is to place the mind inside the heart so that our seeing is not dictated by separateness, division and competition, but by learning how to see the sacredness hidden in the other person, or the aspect of creation that catches our attention. *Blessed are the pure in heart,* says Jesus, *They shall see God.*

This is why Jesus tells us that unless we become like little children, we cannot see the Kingdom of Heaven. It is all about seeing. Children who do not receive the assurance of unconditional love from parents will face life with fear rather than love. This is true for all of us to a greater or lesser degree and may explain why so many Christians are afraid of God and his judgement. Many of us have been brought up to be afraid of going to hell. I recently heard the Franciscan, Richard Rohr, pointing to some teaching of Pope Benedict XVI commenting on the phrase in the Creed, *He descended into hell.* Benedict said that this means that when Christ went down into hell he abolished it.

The spiritual life is not a game of snakes and ladders in which at any point as we move up the ladders we can fall onto a snake and are sent crashing back down. A few years ago I was called to do jury service and I was impressed with the impartiality of the process and the care with which all the members of the jury weighed the evidence. When people ask me about the judgement of God I always say, *Remember that while in a court of law the judge and the jury have to be scrupulously impartial, the God who judges us is passionately in love with us.* Jesus tells his disciples that he will not leave us as orphans when he returns to the Father. He will send us an advocate – the Holy Spirit – someone who is always on our side.

This does not place the Spirit intervening between Jesus on our side and the Father weighing our sins. It is all one. The Spirit who dwells in us is the spirit of Love between the Father and Jesus.

Cleansing the Lens

There is a clear pattern in the bible that God has a preferential love for the poor. Many images underline this preference: the choosing of an enslaved people; the choosing of David; the forgotten son; the barren women and the choice of the young virgin, Mary. Grace and favour are freely given to the unlikely. Mary describes her experience of God as being *looked at* in her unworthiness. The gaze of Infinite Love is always transformative and what Trinitarian mysticism reveals is that God seems vulnerable before our finiteness, he is drawn to our vulnerability. What he seeks from us is a humble *Yes* to just let it be, to allow God to give himself to us, to open our hearts, souls and minds to the divine presence within us.

In contemplative silent prayer we surrender to the unfathomable mystery at work in our deepest being. The gaze of God's love embraces us. In that embrace of Infinite Love we are given the confidence to forget about our unworthiness and our sinfulness and to open ourselves to the gift of unitive consciousness. We are invited to abandon the illusion of our separateness and allow the Infinite Love of Father, Son and Spirit to flow through us as it flows through them. We are transformed from being separate individuals to become persons-in-communion. Our way of seeing is thus transformed from self-referential defensiveness to seeing the image of God, not just in those we love but in the stranger and even the enemy. Paul alludes to this transformation – which is God's work, not ours – in his powerful line, *I live no longer, Christ lives in me.*

What Jesus brought to the world was the ethical responsibility of the Hebrew prophets united with the immediacy of God's presence in his human body. His ethics moved beyond dutiful behaviour to a liberating joy that embraced everyone in the gift of compassion, inclusion and forgiveness.

God was no longer distant, a figure in the sky to be afraid of, but revealed to us in a human face of humble service and extraordinary generosity of spirit. In him the Father's hidden plan was revealed: to bring everything into unity, into unitive consciousness, both in heaven and earth:

> They will see his face and his name will be on their foreheads, and there will be no more night; they need no light or lamp or sun, for the Lord God will be their light.[21]

In the book of Revelation the scriptures then draw to a close with the invitation from the Spirit for all who are thirsty – with desire and longing – to drink freely of the water of life. What Jesus and the mystics tell us is that we can begin to drink this water of life now. Water flows, and this image of flowing water captures the movement, flow and interchange in our Trinitarian God. As this flowing life of love and energy increases within the deepest part of our being, it naturally seeks to flow out into our world and transform it with its healing presence and its effortless joy.

---

21. Rev 22:4-5

7. The Jesus Revolution

You shall be holy, for I the Lord your God am holy.
Leviticus 19:2

Be merciful, just as your Father is merciful.
Luke 6:36

One of the distorted opinions about mysticism is to dismiss it as a private option that provides an escape from the problems of the world. The opposite is in fact true; mysticism is a way of seeing rightly. The journey within is the journey without. It teaches how to look at the world through the eyes of compassion. It is a gift that our fragmented world badly needs. Unhealthy religion has been and still is too often a cause of conflict and violence. We need compassionate seeing.

The non-profit organisation *Technology, Entertainment and Design* (TED) arranges major conferences on *ideas worth spreading.* In 2008, at the request of Karen Armstrong, they coordinated responses from a number of major religions to produce a Charter for Compassion, which would reflect the shared wisdom of major faith traditions with regard to the virtue which is central to all mature religious faith. The initiative generated thousands of replies from all over the world and in several languages including Hebrew, Urdu, Arabic, English and Spanish. The final version was put together by distinguished members of six faith traditions: Judaism; Christianity; Islam; Hinduism; Buddhism and Confucianism. Here is an extract:

> We acknowledge that we have failed to live compassionately and that some have even increased the sum of human misery in the name of religion. We therefore call upon all men and women:

- To restore compassion to the centre of morality and religion
- To return to the ancient principle that any interpretation of scripture that breeds violence, hatred or disdain is illegitimate
- To ensure that youth are given accurate and respectful information about other traditions, religions and cultures
- To encourage a positive appreciation of cultural and religious diversity
- To cultivate an informed empathy with the suffering of all human beings – even those regarded as enemies.

We urgently need to make compassion a clear, luminous and dynamic force in our polarized world. Rooted in a principled determination to transcend selfishness, compassion can breakdown political, dogmatic, ideological and religious boundaries.

Born of our deep interdependence, compassion is essential to human relationships and to a fulfilled humanity. It is the path to enlightenment, and indispensable to the creation of a just economy and a peaceful global community.[22]

Misunderstanding Holiness

The life of Jesus is the outstanding example of a compassionate life. As Christians we need to remind ourselves that Jesus was a Jew and his compassion was rooted in that part of the Hebrew tradition that understood God as compassion. But it wasn't the dominant understanding in Jewish spirituality.

---

22. https://charterforcompassion.org/the-charter

The world that Jesus lived in was dominated by the teaching from Leviticus, *Be holy as God is holy.* Understanding these two interpretations of holiness explains the growing conflict between Jesus and the Jewish religious leaders which we find on almost every page of the gospels. This conflict had both personal and social implications. The social structure of Jewish society at the time of Jesus reflected the dominant paradigm of holiness. So Jesus' critique of this paradigm and his preference for compassion had profound implications which eventually led to his death on the cross.

The problem was created by the Jewish leaders' interpretation of holiness as *separation* from everything unclean. Society was structured along very rigid lines of division and distinction based on what was judged pure and impure, worthy and unworthy, clean and unclean. These divisions applied to all aspects of Jewish society at the time of Jesus: persons, places, things, times and social groups. Priests and Levites headed the hierarchy of the pure and the worthy, followed by circumcised Jewish males, and their superior status was even reflected in the layout of the temple courtyards. Women came further down the pecking order due to menstruation and childbirth, which reinforced their inferior status in a strongly patriarchal society, followed by the sick and disabled. The gospel records Mary going to the synagogue for the ritual purification after giving birth to Jesus. The lepers were treated as untouchables. All foreigners as Gentiles were regarded as inferior and those who collected taxes for the occupying Romans were despised and lumped with sinners and prostitutes. The poor were also viewed as impure and unworthy. Interestingly, the shepherds who appear in the gospel account of the birth of Jesus were probably ranked as social outcasts.

Jesus refused to follow this understanding of holiness as separation. For him, compassion was at the heart both of his message and his lifestyle. He reached out to the poor and the sinners and even dined with them. This was a serious breach of the laws of separation and caused great scandal to the religious leaders. He readily offered forgiveness to sinners and associated with them:

> All the tax-collectors and sinners were coming near to listen to him. And the Pharisees and the scribes were grumbling and saying, *This man welcomes sinners and eats with them.*[23]

Jesus even invited a hated tax-collector into his close circle and dined with him in his home:

> As he sat at dinner in Levi's house, many tax collectors and sinners were also sitting with Jesus and his disciples – for there were many who followed him. When the scribes of the Pharisees saw that he was eating with sinners and tax-collectors, they said to his disciples, *Why does he eat with tax-collectors and sinners?*[24]

One of his most striking breaches of the purity law is recounted by Mark when Jesus meets a leper:

> A leper came to him, begging on his knees, *If you want to you can cleanse me.* Deeply moved, Jesus put out his hand, touched him, and said, *I want to. Be clean.*[25]

Describing Jesus as deeply moved is a way of emphasising the compassion that characterised all his actions. As in everything he was telling us what his Father was really like. In physically touching the leper he was breaking the Jewish law of separation, showing us that God is not interested in separating pure and impure, worthy and unworthy.

---

23. Lk 15:1-2
24. Mk 2:15-17
25. Mk 1:40-41

He was trying to rescue the deeper Jewish tradition of holiness as compassion. In many ways compassion is a maternal quality springing from the womb of a mother. It is a powerful image of God's love for us, like a mother caring deeply for the child of her womb. In Jesus we see God's love as nurturing, life-giving, caring and nourishing. This deep interior love and concern shows also in his relativising of the law of the Sabbath.

Mark relates the incident when the disciples of Jesus picked the ears of corn as they walked through the cornfield. The Pharisees immediately accuse them of breaking the Sabbath law. Jesus replied by placing the law at the service of people not the other way round:

> The Sabbath was made to serve us; we weren't made to serve the Sabbath.[26]

It has often been remarked that Jesus only seemed to work on one day of the week! We never read of him going into Capernaum on a Tuesday afternoon or crossing the lake on a Thursday morning. It is nearly always the Sabbath as Jesus seeks to drive home his attitude to the Law. Jesus was not against the Law; in fact in his Sermon on the Mount he deepened and radicalised it. Compassion wasn't just to be offered to the people we like and approve of; it even reached out to include our enemies.

> You have heard that it was said, *You shall love your neighbour and hate your enemy.* But I say to you, *Love your enemies and pray for those who persecute you, so that you may be children of your Father in heaven;* for he makes his sun to rise on the evil and on the good, and sends his rain on the righteous and the unrighteous.[27]

---

26. Mk 2:27 *The Message* Translation op cit
27. Mt 5:43-45

In this passage Jesus is clearly revealed as a non-dual teacher. No separation of pure and impure, worthy and unworthy, good and bad, righteous and unrighteous.

The inclusiveness and compassion of Jesus also reaches out to women who were second-class citizens in the social system. Not all Jewish teachers subscribed to this view of women but the majority certainly did. Women had few rights: they could not be witnesses in a court of law, they could not begin divorce proceedings, and they were not allowed to study the Torah. They were separated from men in the synagogues with the men taking the more important positions.

Jesus demonstrates a remarkable inclusivity with women. He allows the woman afflicted by haemorrhages to touch him, and heals her rather than scolds her. He respects her dignity as a daughter of Abraham. He defends and praises the intimate demonstration of love by the woman who shocked all the men at an all-male meal in Bethany. He allows the Syro-Phoenecian woman to challenge him not to ignore her. He speaks with great candour with the Samaritan woman with a dubious marital history and reveals his identity to her. He befriends Martha and Mary and many other women who followed him and stood by him on Calvary when the male disciples were conspicuous by their absence. Today we are beginning to rediscover the significance of Mary Magdalene[28] as a close friend and disciple of Jesus despite the fact that her prominence seems to have been written out and obscured in the Early Church. At least the gospels record her importance as witness to the resurrection and her role as *apostle to the apostles.*

---

28. See Cynthia Bourgeault, *Mary Magdalene* (Shambala, Boston 2010)

The Jesus Revolution

Jews in the time of Jesus had their expectations for the predicted Messiah, and most of them involved a political revolution that would drive out the Roman occupiers and restore the kingdom of Israel. Even after his resurrection his apostles asked him, *Is this the time, Lord, when you will restore the kingdom to Israel?* They still had not understood his frequent teaching about the Kingdom of God as his core message. This was not a political kingdom – it was not subject to observation – it was a social and personal transformation which can only be understood as a revolution in consciousness. His teaching about the kingdom is non-dual. He offers inclusive descriptions. He avoids saying it is just like this because *this* would exclude *that*.

Throughout history many revolutions have occurred; very few of them have involved an interior transformation. The new leadership tends to adopt the same old pattern of leadership as domination. Jesus was very critical of this. When pointing out how the rulers of the pagans lord it over their subjects, he gave a stern warning that this must not happen among his followers. The Church with its hierarchical structure has all too frequently forgotten these words. You only have to think of the silencing of theologians and priests and some brave women, who have dared to challenge current teaching about women's ordination. The secrecy of the disciplinary processes seems to pay scant regard to natural justice. The leadership modelled by Jesus was very different. It was servant leadership. The washing of his disciples' feet is the classic example and it is interesting to see how Peter struggled to accept this. Today we are seeing Pope Francis reminding us of this style of servant leadership by words and actions. Some prominent clerics tried to explain away his washing the feet of a young woman in a prison on Maundy Thursday.

The teaching of Jesus in the Sermon on the Mount is subversive of practically everything his contemporaries took for granted. He spoke of turning the other cheek, of loving enemies, of praying for those who attack us. We are encouraged to bless those who curse us and forgive not just seven times, but seventy times. Such teaching if followed out would radically alter all social relations and structures. Equally revolutionary was his turning upside down of the normal relations between rich and poor. While they commonly regarded the poor as cursed, Jesus said they were *blessed*. Where they thought of the rich as *blessed*, Jesus warned them that they would find it very difficult to enter the Kingdom unless they shared their wealth with the poor. Jesus was more concerned with the need for a deep personal change, a real conversion of heart to a life of compassion and service. He knew that without this any change of external structure would not really change anything.

A Change of Consciousness

If we are honest we have to admit that there are aspects of the Sermon on the Mount that pass over our heads. We hear the words and dismiss them as being poetic, not really applying to what we call the real world. What the mystics tell us is that our ordinary way of looking at reality – the egoic operating system – is incapable of seeing reality as it really is. Our ordinary way of looking is locked into the dualism of the binary mindset. We automatically divide what we see into polar opposites:

> good and bad,
> right and wrong,
> black and white,
> heaven and earth,
> body and soul,
> male and female
> and so on.

Contemplation helps us to clarify the lens so that we can drop our defensiveness and our judging minds and see just what *is* as *it is*. Our egoic operating system is not easy to abandon because it wants to place us on a superior plane to others, those we disapprove of. To go beyond our judging calculating mind is much more difficult and challenging than going to Mass, or following The Ten Commandments. Many Christians seem far happier with *an eye for an eye* rather than forgiveness. For us, the radical love and compassion to which Jesus invites us is frankly impossible. We can never achieve perfection. Why is this?

All of us are subject to the human condition. All of us are to some extent flawed. At the same time we are blessed, and the mature spiritual journey consists in the creative holding of this tension between light and dark. When we reflect on the Scribes and Pharisees fighting Jesus over what they considered as the correct understanding of the law and its traditions, we can see that they were still trapped in the first-half-of-life agenda. The task of the first half of life is to build a container as we try to establish ourselves and our identity with an education, a job, a family and a career. Religion with its teachings, practices and rituals helps provide a secure container for this task. It is a healthy way to begin.

Unfortunately many people – including religious believers – never get beyond this stage. They fail to understand that the whole point of building the container is to taste and draw upon the contents. They love the wineskins rather than the wine. They fail to realise that the ego they have busily been building has to die and give way to a much deeper and richer life. They cannot move beyond the separate self. When they experience the inevitable flaws of the human condition they much prefer to attack the flaws of others rather than admit their own failures.

There are still plenty of *Pharisees* about who see the spiritual journey as climbing the ladder of perfection and feeling superior about it. They lack compassion.

The mystics are among those who can guide us through the experience of learning to look at ourselves with compassion and then extending that compassion to others. We begin to taste the wine of life when we grasp the wisdom teaching of Jesus. This encourages us not to be afraid of letting go of the controlling egos and living a life of unitive consciousness, which takes away the need to win the moral struggle to become perfect with effort and will-power. If we wish to see the world through the eyes of Jesus we have to move to unitive consciousness by which we see reality through the eyes of oneness. Jesus describes this Kingdom of God in two great one-liners:

> The Father and I are one.[29]

and

> Whatever you do to the least of my brothers and sisters you do to me.[30]

The Contemplative Gift

Unitive consciousness reveals that the gift of divine indwelling is already given. We do not and cannot earn this by our own efforts. The good news of the gospel is that if we can humbly recognise our failures and limitations, God pours his love into us with compassion and mercy. When we see Jesus healing the sick and the suffering and forgiving sinners, he doesn't ask them about which doctrines they believe in or when they last went to the synagogue. He doesn't judge; he accepts. When he is confronted with the demand to condemn the woman guilty of adultery he refuses and forces her accusers to recognise their own failings.

---

29. Jn 10:30
30. Mt 25:40

Contemplation is not the only path to compassion – great love and great suffering can also get us there. It is a forgotten path for Western Christians which is being rediscovered in our times as our world is changing so rapidly. In order for us to live at the level of union with God and union with others in love and compassion we need some regular practice. We have to move out of our judging minds to the spaciousness of God's Infinite Love and mercy. Too often religious teachers present God as remote and inaccessible, just watching from afar and waiting to punish us. It is not surprising that we see so much atheism and agnosticism in the West. We have failed to proclaim the radical grace of the gospel. We have failed to grasp the astonishing truth of the Incarnation: that God came into our world and said this is where you will find me. Jesus showed us how to find God in imperfection rather than perfection. That is the Jesus revolution.

A regular practice of contemplation teaches us how to accept reality for what it is. Instead of judging ourselves and others we learn to accept *what is*, to look with compassionate rather than judgemental eyes. Eastern mysticism has long taught how to do this. It teaches how to look at and recognise the patterns in all our thoughts and emotions as they pass through our awareness during meditation. When we receive criticism we very quickly slip into well-used story lines that trigger negative emotions and judgements. The Eastern masters talk about finding *a stable witness* from which to calmly observe these mental processes. Such an exercise helps the necessary detachment from these thoughts and emotions.

As Christians we do not have to find a stable witness because Jesus has given us the Holy Spirit, the advocate, the defender, the one who is always on our side. We do not even have to open ourselves to this forgiving flow of the Spirit;

it flows freely into us. In contemplative prayer we discover that we do not have to cling on to God. We are always and objectively being held by the continuous flow of giving and receiving love that we call Father, Son and Spirit.

That is why mystics such as Julian of Norwich can say that, *All shall be well*, and Thomas Merton can say that *The cosmic dance goes on* and we don't have to beat our brains trying to figure it all out. The invitation is to join in the dance. God has planted a homing device in the deepest core of our being that is always connected to the Great Love, the Great River of Mercy, the Body of Christ in which *all things* are reconciled. We learn to laugh as we become present to this moment just as it is and we can learn to weep as we become present to another moment. To laugh or to weep is to move beyond judgment.

In trying to live a contemplative life we become more attuned to this flowing energetic presence. We begin to see the divine image in others before we start critiquing and judging. We discover and increasingly enjoy the truth that God is perfectly hidden and perfectly revealed in everything.

Non-dual Leadership

When Nelson Mandela died tributes came from all over the world, from political leaders and religious leaders across the spectrum. Former President Bill Clinton described him as a man of uncommon grace and compassion. Archbishop Desmond Tutu referred to him as a unifier. The Indian Prime minister called him a true Gandhian. Others referred to him as a man who chose reconciliation over retribution, forgiveness over bitterness and someone who knew how to play, dance and radiate joy.

I recall listening to him on the BBC speaking about his long imprisonment. He said, *Prison taught me so much*. Mandela teaches our cynical and often violent world that non-dual leadership can work. Forged in the crucible of suffering he emerged as a leader able to reconcile opposites, love his enemies and bring forth a deeper truth of a common humanity.

8. The Mystery of Paradox

> The purpose of paradox...is not to deny or destroy the human mind with nonsense but to bring the normal human intellect to the awareness of its own limitations, and thus open up to the possibility of a higher kind of knowing.[31]
>
> *Cyprian Smith OSB*

The mystical path takes us beyond the limitations of the rational mind into a new way of seeing. It is a wisdom that is not easy to articulate in our capitalist culture and mindset and the logic of Western philosophy. It takes us into the world of contradictions and ambiguity. The word *contradiction* refers to things that appear to be mutually exclusive or inconsistent according to our present frame of logic, or point of view. The problem with first-half-of-life religion is that the container we so carefully constructed to survive the inconsistencies that we meet everywhere – and particularly inside ourselves – cannot get us beyond these contradictions. We are forced to deny or shift the blame to someone else: to a member of my community, or my family, or another race, another country or another gender. We don't want to acknowledge *the pain body* that we carry within ourselves, all the failures, the shameful side of life, the insecurities we feel, the lack of worthiness.

Unhealthy religion doesn't know how to deal with this pain so it simply generates more guilt. This explains why so many adults walk away from institutional religion. The whole purpose of religion is to teach us how to live with and be transformed by what we think are the great obstacles in the spiritual life. It offers us a different mindset. It invites us into the contemplative mind.

---

31. Cyprian Smith OSB, *The Way of Paradox*, (Darton, Longman & Todd,London 2011) p27

This is the new software that teaches a new way of seeing, what Cyprian Smith calls a *higher form of knowing*. Contemplative seeing reveals that contradictions are not a threat to the spiritual life, they are a necessary part of it. We are not asked to abandon our rational, critical mind, but to *sharpen* it. We begin to learn that A and B can indeed both be true at a much deeper level.

The wisdom of paradox takes us to a deeper place beyond the simple certainties of black and white opinions to include both *knowing* and *not knowing*. Whenever the Church and theologians have sought to reduce faith to clearly-stated certainties, the mystics have always reminded us that we can never fully grasp the Holy Mystery that we call God. Consider the two great appearances of God in the Bible on Mount Sinai and Mount Tabor. When Moses seeks intimacy with God he is enveloped by divine light but a cloud covers the top of the mountain. When Jesus is transfigured on Mount Tabor his clothes radiate light but again a cloud appears to block the view of Peter, James and John. The message is clear to Moses, the apostles, and to all of us: don't ever presume that you have seen it all. The point is clear: we cannot get to God on our own, we cannot grab hold of God, we are in fact held by God. The spiritual journey is not an obstacle course, a series of moral hoops that we have to jump through, it is a relational mystery. At the heart of this mystery is the deepest and most profound intimacy and union possible. We discover that everyone and everything is included in this mystery. It is essentially a mystery of connection and participation.

This mystery of connection and participation is not a detailed plan, a blueprint for holiness. It is much more a process, a way of seeing, that leads to a transformation of consciousness. Jesus doesn't tell us *what* to see but *how* to see, how to see reality.

In our egocentric mind we are programmed to try to fit everything into our own separate and limited point of view. Jesus presents us with a series of paradoxes that stretch and break open that narrow egocentric way of looking at reality and take us into the spacious mystery of the Kingdom of God. Richard Rohr[32] draws out a number of these challenging paradoxes from the life and teaching of Jesus. Finding is losing, losing is finding. The poor are rich, the rich are poor. Weeping is bliss, bliss is weeping. Meekness is possession, possession is emptiness. Death is real life, life is about dying. Death and resurrection cannot be separated. The wise and the learned do not understand, little children do. Folly is wisdom, the wise are ignorant. Weakness is strength, strength is weakness. These are all teachings that cannot be understood by the binary mind.

Soul Connection

The task of religion is to lead us into these rich paradoxes and to learn how to sit patiently until they reveal their deeper truth. When speaking in the United States, the Dalai Lama is said to have wept when someone asked him if there was a quick way to enlightenment. Our culture today is kept at a superficial level by the sheer volume of information and entertainment thrown at us. Our smart phones offer us instant and immediate access to everything that is happening. We see people walking the streets glued to their phone screens unable to see what is before their eyes. Twenty-four hour news bulletins promise to bring us the latest information on everything that is happening. What are we supposed to do with this information overload? The Queen of England warned us in her annual Christmas message for 2013 about the need for a new balance between action and reflection in our lives, the need for a more *contemplative* way of looking at reality.

---

32. Richard Rohr, *Holding the Tension. The Power of Paradox*, (CD Agape Ministries, Southport.)

This gap between levels of information provided by our ever more sophisticated technology and the need for quiet reflection is the reason why more people are turning to the mystics and the revival of the contemplative tradition. Living a connected life has to go beyond a superficial consumption of information to a deeper connection at the level of soul. Technology is not bad; it is a question of how we use it. In fact technology has opened us up to the reality of what is happening in our world. It may be providing endless sources of entertainment but at the same time it can inform us about the wars and conflicts of our time. It informs us about the plight of refugees. It informs us about the natural disasters such as earthquakes or tsunamis that afflict our planet. It informs us about the melting of the polar ice-caps and other threats to the environment.

Facing the many crises of our world our political leaders often seem trapped in trying to respond. The same is true of many of our religious leaders whose seeing is too often reduced to short-sightedness. We don't see the bigger picture. If we are indeed entering a new axial age the question of how we see becomes central. Carl Jung prophetically pointed out that in this modern age we need to find and recover our souls. The dualism of recent centuries can no longer be the primary way we look at the world. We have to find a way beyond the oppositional thinking of who is right and who is wrong, conservative or liberal, of all-or-nothing thinking, of us and them. We need to recover the underlying unity at the root of all reality. After 2000 years of Christianity it is disappointing that we Christians have often lost the treasure within, the pearl of great price that is contemplative seeing. Thankfully, the saints and the mystics kept it alive for us and it is emerging in many parts of the world today as we face the challenges of the future.

An Inclusive Consciousness

Past revolutions and reformations have often reinforced the dualistic mindset of we are right and they are wrong. The cry of liberty and fraternity in France ended in the guillotine. The Russian revolution, promising a new utopia of socialism to help the poor, ended in repression of any opposition in the gulags. I recall standing on the beaches of Liberia in West Africa where the triumphant revolutionaries had executed their predecessors. You might think that religious reformations would do it better, but during the Reformation Protestant Christians tortured and killed Catholic Christians, and vice versa. Today we witness bitter rivalry and violence between Christians and Muslims in the Central African Republic and in South Sudan. At the time of writing this book, The Tate Gallery in London is staging an exhibition of damaged art entitled *Art Under Attack,* from the 16th century, featuring the destruction of Catholic art by the reformers to the present day. It includes art damaged for religious, political or aesthetic reasons and tries to uncover the motivations for such attacks. Whatever they might be, I suspect the dualistic mind is at the root of many of these destructive acts, and it is sad to see religious dualism featuring so strongly.

Any belief system that cannot deal with paradox will attract the immature. Such either/or thinking will not only produce destructive behaviour it also affects individual lives. A refusal to admit and deal with contradictions and paradoxes will produce unhappy people. It is impossible to be really happy if I am constantly judging, condemning or dismissing others. Shadow suppression is a serious block to mature growth. Christianity seems to have struggled to find a way of integrating the shadow into the path of holiness as wholeness.

Light and Dark

Jesus was clearly aware of the shadow side of our humanity when he warns us against trying to take the splinter out of our brother's eye while refusing to take the plank out of our own. The invitation to anyone without sin to cast the first stone at the woman taken in adultery is another powerful example. Despite this clear teaching, Christian moral teachers have not found it easy to integrate the dark with the light. We have tended to replicate the rigidity of the Pharisees and fall into the trap of seeing holiness as the path to perfection. We forgot about the Father who lets his sun shine on good and bad, just and unjust alike. Once again we meet the problem of dualism, of separating good from bad, of placing ourselves on the side of righteousness while condemning those we judge unworthy.

Jesus was fully prepared to enter the darkness. After having addressed God with the intimate word *Abba* throughout his life it is almost impossible to comprehend his cry for help on the Cross: *My God, why have you abandoned me?* In his gospel John teaches us that this was the moment marking the reconciliation of all things, *When I am lifted up from the earth I shall draw all things to myself.* For John the death of Jesus is the revealing of his glory. At the moment of greatest darkness the veil of the temple is torn in two and we see the face of God as forgiveness and inclusion. It is not a case of God demanding suffering as the price of reconciliation. It is that wherever suffering exists and is *consciously accepted,* there God's reconciling love is revealed. We see this in our own experience in the most constricting circumstances. When we see the Mizen family in London forgiving the murderer of their son Jimmy, when we see Dee Walker in Liverpool forgiving the murderer of her son, Anthony, when we see Gordon Wilson forgiving the murder of his daughter in Enniskillen, when we see Nelson Mandela forgiving the cruel oppressors of the apartheid regime in South Africa, there we see an extraordinary reconciling love emerging.

There is a further point to be made. Our creed tells us that Jesus *descended into hell.* This has been unconvincingly interpreted as him having to rescue Abraham, Moses, David and all the great spiritual leaders of Israel on the naïve assumption that nobody could enter heaven unless they had been baptised. I think we can safely leave that theory behind and seek a much deeper meaning. What this phrase may be saying is that in the profound letting-go of his life, in accepting the agony and pain of his unjust and cruel death, Jesus is able to reach down into the very depths of darkness and evil and envelop and embrace it with his healing love. In her *Wisdom Jesus,* Cynthia Bourgeault draws on the wisdom tradition to claim that in this act Jesus confronted the powers and principalities of evil and changed the footing on which our present world exists. This is what it means to be saved by the death of Jesus, not a sadistic Father demanding the blood of his Son, but an act of healing and forgiving love which is the salvation of the world.

Bourgeault stresses the necessity of paradox in revealing the nature of God. By becoming flesh Jesus brings the infinite into the constriction of a finite being in a finite world, a world of jagged edges and vulnerability. Our world is both blessed and broken. It contains breathtaking beauty and joy alongside ugliness and pain. All our moments of joy and love are tinged with impermanence, and even sadness. We witness great acts of heroism, love and service alongside selfish greed and cruel violence. I am always struck by the gifts that are brought to the child Jesus by the wise men. These wisdom figures bring gold, frankincense and myrrh.

The gold recognises the splendour of our being, in the recognition that we are brought into this world as partakers in the divine nature. This is far beyond anything we could ever attain by effort and will-power. The gift of myrrh, used to anoint the dead, is a reminder that our life unfolds under the shadow of death and can be marked by sorrow and pain. What holds these two together is the gift of frankincense. This is the gift of prayer and of *consciousness,* the gift that allows us to hold the tension and live joyfully inside all the contradictions and paradoxes of our human condition and our flawed world.

Presence and Participation

When the mystics speak of God as the *Eternal Now* they are teaching about presence. Presence is always an embrace of paradox, of light and dark. We cannot be truly present with the mind. Whenever Jesus meets people in the gospels he doesn't preach generic moral rules. He always meets *this* man, *this* woman, *this* child. Presence is not the same as knowing. We have to recover the kind of seeing and meeting that touches a deeper level of being, before our judging minds take over. Otherwise we will never learn anything new. Theologian Karl Rahner says that we are infinite beings because we are open to more. There is a longing and hunger for mystery in all of us.

We are living through transitional times and our global connectedness is revealing something about this phase of human history. We have grown through pre-rational times when access to the divine was mediated through the powers of myths, to the modern rational world that we live in which has largely sought to debunk all these myths. The next move is into the *transrational* when we can't prove the mystery that enfolds us but we do want to experience it.

The transrational consciousness of the coming age will include both the power of myth and the power of reason. We don't jettison reason, but we learn that it can only take us so far. We have to learn how to live within the tension of opposites, in what the mystics call *infinite ignorance,* or *the cloud of unknowing,* or *luminous darkness.* Bonaventure spoke of the distinction between rational intelligence and what he called sapiential being. This word has the same root as the Spanish *sabor* which means to taste. The mystics always invite us to taste the goodness of the Lord. It is not the cold analysis of the intellect but a knowing that has to be personally experienced in the depth of our being. In contemplative practice our souls are opened up in a loving spaciousness that can receive all things.

In Western Christianity we have tended to emphasise the importance of the *logos* when speaking of God. This has been prominent in the kataphatic tradition. Today we are opening ourselves to include the importance of *sophia,* the traditional word for wisdom. Wisdom takes us beyond the analytical mind to a place of encounter which involves presence, tenderness and vulnerability. The dualistic mind will keep you trapped in the right-brain/left-brain attitude, clearly favouring the left brain. Today we are flooded with information overload and it is not taking us into the challenges of the future. We need time to empty ourselves, to experience silence, even solitude from time to time, so that we can be fully present in moments of engagement. In past centuries mysticism has been kept alive in the deserts, monasteries and hermitages of the world. Today it is emerging all over the world in the dawn of a new consciousness, non-dual, unitive, whatever you want to call it, but one that is radically inclusive of all religions, all cultures, all races as the basis for the new axial age.

The contemplative mind can lead us into this future by teaching us how to accept the contradictions and paradoxes that we all are. We learn how to see the truth wherever we find it. This is seeing with the eye of the heart, what Meister Eckhart called the wisdom-eye. As this eye opens wider we can see all the contraries contained in love and forgiveness. Egocentric consciousness cannot do this; we have to die to the private separate self. We rise to a new self that can live within the tension of right and wrong, good and bad, silence and speech, action and contemplation, engagement and withdrawal, life and death, unity and difference, cross and resurrection.

In his book *The Sign of Jonah,* Thomas Merton described his life as full of paradoxes and he had reached the stage beyond needing to keep apologising for that fact. He reflects that it is in these paradoxes which have caused him most uncertainty, that he has found his greatest security. He has learned to see the contradictions as signs of God's mercy. There are echoes here of one of the great paradoxes referred to by the mystics. They describe their experience of God as a falling into an *abyss* which is at the same time the *ground* of mercy. Elsewhere Merton maintains that mercy is the deepest thing that has been revealed to us by God.

Our culture does so much to protect and promote the separate self. The irony is that we only discover our true identity when we find ourselves in the abyss of God's mercy. There we discover ourselves in the other and the other in us. We can move beyond *I am* and *I have* language into the great I AM that we all are in God.

9. One with Creation

In the beginning was the Word and the Word was with God, and the Word was God. He was in the beginning with God. All things came into being through him, and without him not one thing came into being. What has come into being through him was life, and the life was the light of all people. The light shines in the darkness and the darkness could not overcome it.

John 1:1-5

In the morning, while it was still very dark, he got up and went to a very deserted place, and there he prayed.

Mark1:35

As a young boy growing up, I loved football. My brother and I would collect autographs of our favourite players. If I had been alive in the time of Jesus and asked him for his autograph he would not have written Jesus Christ. His name was Jesus, and Christ was not his surname. Jesus Christ combines a name and a title. In the Early Church Jesus was increasingly called *The Christ,* which means *The Anointed One* or *The Lord.* As the prologue of John's gospel makes clear The Christ existed timelessly before creation while Jesus was born into earth's time. Jesus was a Jew; Christ was not. Paul in his writings rarely speaks of Jesus; for him it is always Christ. As Christians, not surprisingly, we have fallen in love with Jesus. Unfortunately we tend to forget that Jesus was more concerned that we follow him rather than worship him. He didn't even want to be made King of Israel. When he was addressed as, *Good Master* he asked, *Why?* For Jesus, only God was good. He sets before us a much more challenging path than feeling good about ourselves: he told us that in order to gain the fullness of life we have to die to some part of ourselves.

Necessary Suffering

There is no doubt that many of the mystics focus strongly on the sufferings of Jesus. We find this in people like Julian of Norwich, who even as a young girl, asked for the grace of a serious illness before the age of thirty. This might seem a strange request to us but it reveals her intuitive grasp of the necessity of some kind of dying to the first-half-of-life agenda. She understood what Jesus meant when he insisted that we have to lose our life in order to truly save it. Jesus had to die in order to become the Christ and we have to follow the same path. What we have to die to is our small, individual, separate, egocentric self – so that we can discover and live from our True Self. Like Jesus we have to discover our true life in Christ.

This is not just a religious issue; it affects not only human life but the whole of creation. Carl Jung observed that so much suffering occurs in people's lives because they will not accept the necessary suffering that comes from simply being human. We all struggle with this apparently hard message, but we see it laid bare – if we have eyes to see – in creation. Even our sun is dying as it transforms itself into light so that we can live. Creation is living what we call *The Paschal Mystery* each day, each season and each year, in the rhythm of dying and the emergence of new life. Francis of Assisi intuited this deep connection with all creation when he referred to Brother Sun and Sister Moon, while at the same time being so conscious of the suffering path of Jesus that he carried the marks of his passion on his own body. This is not a masochistic message. Julian, Francis, John of the Cross and many other mystics lived lives of great joy and love because their suffering, their dying, had brought them into union with God, with others and with all of nature. Their mystical hearts were big enough to hold the tension between the joys and sorrows of life.

The message is not easy, and yet it should be central to the teaching of the Church. For many centuries the dominant theological opinion of the atonement has viewed the suffering and death of Jesus as a ransom payment to God for human sin. This has done great damage. Fortunately there has always been a minority theological opinion held by many others, such as Duns Scotus, Francis of Sales and others, who rejected the idea that the Incarnation was a mopping-up exercise. It is far more wonderful and liberating than that. The Incarnation is the high point of creation and it is revealed in the joining of matter and spirit. This is the unified field that we seek, the Big Picture that holds everything together in saving love. It rests on the astonishing heart of the good news: that Jesus became human so that we would discover our divinity. There is an extraordinary moment in every Eucharist during the Offertory when the priest adds a drop of water into the chalice of wine and he says these words:

> By the mystery of this water and wine may we come to share in the divinity of Christ who humbled himself to share in our humanity.

That is why we have been created.

From the Newtonian world of separation to the Quantum Theory of connection

The First Axial Age led to a strong emergence of the individual rather than the collective. The rise of science and technology in recent centuries has further strengthened the position of the autonomous individual, as evidenced by the choice of Frank Sinatra's *My Way* as a favourite funeral song. Because much of our theology and spirituality was trapped in the dualistic world view, the Church accepted the prevailing mythos of the time. For Isaac Newton, in the seven-teenth century, the whole universe was a great machine.

He believed in a God who just started the whole thing by winding it up like a gigantic clock and then left it to run. The universe was a collection of objects, the smallest of which were atoms. Everything operated by the strict laws of physics. We were left with a universe (and a God) that was orderly, hierarchical, perfect and unchangeable. The spiritual journey involved climbing a ladder to get to heaven which was up in the skies above (a view regularly illustrated by sports stars today after scoring a goal, or a touchdown). As science and technology has increasingly shaped our lives, God was more and more sidelined. He became the god of the gaps. The dualistic, rational, binary mind took over the interpretation of reality. Contemplation largely disappeared from the scene. For many people prayer only features in their lives as a last resort when they hit problems.

Today we are witnessing a revolution in how we view the universe, and it is proving very exciting and challenging for spiritual teachers and practitioners. It involves a real paradigm shift. It demonstrates that we are not objective observers of a static, unchanging universe, but we are active participants in a continuously emerging universe. When we saw those astonishing pictures of our planet from space it changed everything. The discovery that we live in an evolving rather than a static universe has profound implications, not only for how we view the world and creation but how we view God. Today we can say that the universe is in a continuing process of transformation, of dying to new life, which mirrors the spiritual path known as The Paschal Mystery.

While Newton's view saw objects as solid and disconnected, the world of quantum physics tells a very different tale. Einstein, and others after him, opened up the atom to discover a range of particles such as electrons, protons and neutrons right down to the smallest quarks. They could not be described as particles or waves or anything that could be objectified, but they demonstrated patterns of behaviour. There are so many puzzling aspects of quantum behaviour which defy our rational logical minds. The scientist, Nils Bohr, suggested that if we are not confused or shocked by the quantum world we have not understood it. It is a world in which elementary particles can behave as both particles and waves depending how we view them. The quantum world is nothing like the world we live in. It is fundamentally mysterious. Even the great genius Albert Einstein was taken aback when his work led him to the discovery that the universe was expanding in all directions. He even falsified some of his equations to safeguard the view that the universe was fixed. Some years later Edwin Hubble invited Einstein to look through his telescope and see the truth of his original findings.

As well as being a mysterious universe it is also an uncertain one as the *Principle of Uncertainty* reveals. We cannot easily predict the future in this evolving world, we can only guess at probabilities. It is a participatory universe. We are not spectators in this world we are actors and participants. The most important aspect of this quantum world view is the fact that everything is inter-connected. So when Jesus and the mystics speak about the underlying oneness and unity of all things they were not just being poetic. Thomas Merton expressed this unity when he declared that, *We are already one and what we have to become is what we are already are*. You can see why the mystics speak about unitive consciousness. Creation is not a thing; it is a relationship. To be created is to be related. Ken Wilber describes us as *holons*, not isolated parts but parts that contain the whole. All beings are holons, distinct modes of being (wholes) that are parts of a more complex mode of being. Inter-connectedness lies at the heart of everything that exists.

David Bohm uses the phrase *implicate order* to express this connection. He is a good example of a modern scientist who is open to the reality of the spiritual. He sees the universe as implicated, that is folded up together, and what we see in our everyday world is the explicate order, what has been and is being unfolded. The implicate order is continually being unfolded, becoming explicate. It appears to the rational mind that we are all separate individuals. In fact our roots are part of an indivisible whole and we all share in the same cosmic process. There is an increasing amount of scientific evidence to move us from the mechanistic world view to a new holistic and ecological one. We are all interconnected and interdependent. Our universe is in an evolving dynamic process and we are a conscious part of it. The notion of an implicate order moves us from our exclusive concentration on externals to the inner relational quality which flows through all things.

The British scientist Rupert Sheldrake speaks of *morphogenetic fields.* He claims that systems are surrounded by non-visible fields that hold the memory of and carry information about previous learning patterns. Just think of how quickly young children pick up computer skills so much faster than older generations. As more and more people do something, the easier it becomes for others to learn it. Like influences like, with what Sheldrake calls *morphic resonance.* Although Jesus would never have spoken about morphic fields of influence, his whole mission was about creating such a field of influence dominated not by power but by love. His phrase for this was *The Kingdom of God.* His chief concern was not the next world, but how to live in this one. As we have seen earlier this was an inclusive kingdom based on compassion, love, forgiveness and mercy.

This was a direct challenge to the purity codes of his time. This challenge to the strict separatist codes of contemporary Judaism led to his death. For Jesus, love as compassion was rooted in the deep connectivity of how he experienced his Father, as Abba. This led to his radical inclusion of the Other and his love of the world of nature, where he so frequently prayed and felt at home.

In the very first chapter of Mark's gospel, as Jesus is just beginning his mission, he invites a small group to join him, Simon and his brother Andrew, James and his brother John. Practically every founder invites their followers to live in community. Hermits are rare in religious life but interestingly they are re-appearing in the Church, as the mystical path is being rediscovered for our times. Such solitaries are mature men or women who have usually spent several years in community. For most people, spirituality grows in families or communities because it is essentially relational.

Another important dimension of the new scientific paradigm is the discovery of *Deep Time*. The Big Bang occurred 13.7 billion years ago. If you consider the Encyclopaedia of Life as an evolving story, it has thirty volumes each with 450 pages with each page representing one million years. The universe begins with the Big Bang in volume one. The earth appears in volume twenty one. Life appears in volume twenty two. The Cambrian period with the advent of the dinosaurs appears in volume twenty nine. The dinosaurs become extinct on page 385 of volume thirty. The mammals are extinct on page 390. On page 450, of volume thirty, human beings appear on the very last page. The story continues with us. What we call *homo sapiens* has been around for about 0.04% of earth's existence. The modern human physique first emerged in Africa 150,000 years ago. All this puts our lives in perspective.

Evolution of Consciousness

The key to understanding our role in the great scheme of things is *the evolution of consciousness* as Teilhard de Chardin pointed out in the last century. We are the universe come to conscious awareness. We can give voice to all of creation. What is significant today is the shift in consciousness that is taking place in our times. We have seen how human persons developed a sense of individual, separate existence in the first axial age. Theology and spirituality largely echoed this sense of who we were. We are now emerging from the high point of this world view with our science and technology. The general sense of many people today is of fragmentation, indicating a time of chaos. We are afflicted by so many crises, political, economic, ecological and religious. Many of our institutions are failing to cope. Religion which should provide some wisdom seems to be as much a part of the problem as the solution with its wars and conflicts, the crisis of sexual abuse among the clergy and the lack of young people attending churches.

If we read the signs of the times there is no doubt that a new consciousness is arising. Alongside all the discoveries of cosmology, Western psychology has now opened up to the spiritual. Jung was something of a pioneer in this field but great strides are being made today in the field of transpersonal psychology with a particular focus on the development of consciousness. Experts in this field such as Ken Wilber, Don Beck, Richard Rohr and Bill Plotkin are using modern language to open the kind of ground explored by mystics such as Teresa of Ávila, in her *Interior Castle*, and John of the Cross with his *Dark Nights of the Soul*. What these transpersonal teachers are teaching is that there are different levels of maturity in the spiritual journey.

While they may disagree as to the number of levels, what they all agree on is that growth in consciousness is a movement from dualistic levels to non-dual or unitive consciousness. Hence the emergence of the mystics. Where non-dual consciousness was often rare in past centuries, today it is emerging all over the world in the lives of many people. On a cautionary note it is important not to get too caught up in trying to identify different levels, because that appeals to the ego. But they are useful indicators as to the move away from dualistic thinking and reading of reality.

For Christians, it was Teilhard de Chardin who first suggested the need for a coming together of science and religion in this area. He saw the person of Christ as central. For him evolution is all about consciousness as it continues to grow in ever greater complexity. Jesus became human inserting the divine into the human, uniting matter and spirit. His body like ours emerged from the same cosmic dust, but in Jesus something new emerged into our world: a new consciousness, a new relatedness, a new intimacy with God who is addressed as, *Abba, Father.* Maybe this can give us a new understanding of the traditional Catholic teaching on the virgin birth. If Jesus is human and divine, his birth marked a totally new emergence in the human story, a breaking in of something entirely new. Jesus himself told us not to put his teaching into old patterns. New wine, new wineskins! He came into our world as a non-dual teacher with a message that everything is one; one with God, one with his brothers and sisters, and one with creation. He asked us to change our mindset and to see everything with a new heart. The task of humanity is to be this creative heart of love, compassion, mercy and forgiveness in the world. In the tradition of the Hebrew prophets he joined ethical responsibility to a heart and mind in constant and intimate union with his Father.

What emerged in Jesus was the immediacy and clarity of God's love, forgiveness, a healing presence, and with the death and resurrection of Jesus he became the Christ figure for all of creation.

This new unitive consciousness is changing the way we look upon different religions. For too long in humanity's history, religion has been contained within a tribal consciousness and this has always been a strong feature of the first axial age. The Franciscan Sister, Ilia Delio,[33] to whom I am greatly indebted for much of the material in this chapter, describes this new consciousness as a new *Catholic* consciousness, that is inclusive rather than exclusive, and leads to greater compassion, reconciliation, mercy and forgiveness. Jesus told his followers to be known by their fruits and in these evolutionary days we are challenged to overcome divisions, not by forcing everyone to become a Catholic, but by allowing the truth of the other to emerge from a perspective of relational oneness.

One important discovery of the universe not yet referred to is the phenomenon of *black holes*. We know very little about these remnants of failed stars. What scientists do know seems to suggest that there is one in every galaxy, even our own Milky Way. The terminology has become part of our everyday vocabulary when we talk of a black hole in a government's spending plans. It was once thought that nothing could emerge from a black hole but the work of Stephen Hawking suggests the possibility of an escape. He maintains that light can even overcome the darkness of a black hole.

---

33. Ilia Delio, *The Emergent Christ* (Orbis Books Maryknoll, NY 2011)
   The Humility of God (St Anthony Messenger Press, Cincinnati, Ohio, 2005)

Judy Cannato in *Radical Amazement* suggests that we can use the term *black hole* to describe the darkest moments of our lives. We can all experience a personal black hole when we lose our job, or a relationship or a marriage breaks down, or someone we love contracts a serious or debilitating illness. We may find ourselves in the grip of a particular addiction. We may fail to properly integrate the shadow side of our life which continues to keep us fighting the battles of the first half of life. For many the black hole experience is a failure to live a fully conscious life. We are trapped in disconnection from the light of life.

How can we deal with these challenging situations in our lives? We have to reach for the light of grace, the light of love that is the very energy of God's creation. This is the gift of contemplation. A regular practice of contemplation opens the core of our being to the radiant love that flows through the whole of creation. Jesus called himself *the light of the world*. When we enter what Jesus calls our inner room we learn to see through the darkness and pain of all human suffering. We begin to touch the peace that the world cannot give. What we thought was just darkness reveals the light of Christ, the Jesus who, as the risen Christ, is bringing everything together and making everything new.

10. A Relational God

> For in him all the fullness of God was pleased to dwell, and through him God was pleased to reconcile to himself all things, whether on earth or in heaven, by making peace through the blood of his cross.
>
> *Colossians 1:19-20*
>
> Examine yourselves to see whether you are living in the faith. Test yourselves. Do you not realise that Jesus Christ is in you?
>
> *2 Corinthians 13:5*

If we are entering into a new axial age, it is important to ask what is empowering this great transition and development. My suggestion in this book is that we are experiencing a growth in consciousness. We are being invited to move from a predominantly tribal and ethno-centric consciousness – *my country, my race, my religion* – to a more world-centric awareness. What the mystics have intuited over the centuries is becoming more evident as we move into a new future. As we have grown more connected electronically and economically, we are seeing signs of a spirituality that seeks to find meaning in the profound changes we are currently undergoing and in the underlying unity of all things. The increasing use of the word *ecology* is moving us away from the sense of separateness from nature as we have exploited the planet. The sense that we are deeply connected with everything – *with God, with others, and with creation* – is much more in tune with our times. Where previously science and religion have been on separate paths, we are now hearing our scientists tell us that all aspects of the universe from the smallest particle to the largest galaxies are connected. Science and religion have joined to tell us that we are living in a relational world.

The specific contribution of Christians to this shift in perspective is the growing reflection by a number of theologians on the central Christian mystery of the Trinity. Karl Rahner famously said that if the doctrine of the Trinity were to be eliminated from Christian thinking, it would make little practical difference to the lives of most Christian believers. This is not the fault of ordinary believers. It is a result of a rather speculative theological history that has taken this profound central mystery out of the realm of everyday life by placing it in a theological bubble. This is a long way from the brilliance of St Paul's intuitive grasp of the centrality of this mystery. The quotes at the head of this chapter underline the reconciling mission of Christ and the fact that Christ is not up there sitting on a cloud in the heavens but is intimately connected with the depths of our being and bringing all things into unity, not by eliminating differences but by reconciling them. A number of highly respected theologians are helping to unpack aspects of this central mystery. They see the relevance not just for Christian believers, but for the way we understand all reality as it continues to unfold from the Creator God that Jesus called, *Abba, Father.*

From Substance to Relationship

In 1991 Catherine LaCugna published the book *God for Us: The Trinity and Christian Life.*[34] It received the Catholic Press Association's first-place award for theology, and it has been credited as almost single-handedly rescuing the mystery of the Trinity from the margins and bringing it back into the mainstream. She sets out the historical process by which the view of the Trinity as a participation in God's redemptive and reconciling love at the heart of all creation has been diminished in favour of abstract and static speculation on the inner life of God.

34. *God for Us: The Trinity and Christian Life.* (HarperSanFrancisco, 1991)

By the fourth century a clear split had occurred between what was called the economic trinity (the action of God in our world) and the theological trinity which covered the inner life of God. Early Christian theology and philosophy was formulated through the cultural prisms of Greek and Roman thought and it is still limited by that constriction.

Aristotle was a key figure in Western Philosophy and he spoke of the difference between substance and relationship. Substance became the dominant idea. It represents independence, autonomy, standing alone like a tree or a chair. So God was substance rather than relationship. Yet for Jesus, in the gospels, God was primarily a relationship as he so often reminded his disciples:

> Do you not believe that I am in the Father
> and the Father is in me?[35]

Western thought preferred the self-made man. Augustine said that God is three substances in one. Contrast that with a mystic like Catherine of Genoa who claimed, *My deepest me is God.* Catherine LaCugna made a passionate case, like her mentor Karl Rahner, to unite the inner life of God with the outer life of salvation. She saw them as two aspects of one reality which she called *the mystery of divine-human communion.* So, for her, the doctrine of the Trinity is an eminently practical teaching that reveals not only how we can understand God, but also how we human beings are created to live in loving awareness of this deeply relational mystery: called to live in communion with the Father who has created us, and the Son who has redeemed us, in the love of the Spirit.

---

35. Jn. 14:10

Because of this relational stress, current theologians such as Beatrice Bruteau, Richard Rohr, Cynthia Bourgeault, Ilia Delio and Michael Downey emphasise the connection between our human attempts to live lives of communion, reconciliation, forgiveness, peace, wonder, non-violence and ecological awareness with the very life and shape of God. It is this creative energy of love that is poured into our hearts that helps to build what Jesus called *The Kingdom of God*, to create what the quantum scientists call a morphogenetic field, a field of compassion, a field of love. They wish to unite the *mysterium tremendum* of Rudolph Otto – the God who dwells in inaccessible light – with the face of God that we see in Jesus, who reveals to us the closeness and the intimacy of the God who is now present not just to Christians but to the whole cosmos. The Risen Christ is present to us in the very core of our being through the power of the Holy Spirit. Wherever there is love there is God.

The Western emphasis on God as substance left us with a God who fitted into the monarchical, hierarchical pattern of the Roman and Medieval World. It was a different story in the Eastern Church led by the fourth century Cappadocian Fathers, Basil, his brother Gregory of Nyssa and his close friend Gregory Nazianzan who emphasised the relational aspect. They approached the Trinity as three that were also one rather than beginning with the one.

The beauty of starting with the three persons is the stress it places on relationships. If God is love, then love must flow and the Father pours himself into the Son who receives and gives back this love to the Father, in and through the Spirit.

We will never grasp this extraordinary mystery with our minds but we can certainly connect with and live in communion with a relational God who enters our world by making himself humble and vulnerable, waiting patiently for our response. Like attracts like and love attracts love.

All we have to do is to participate in the endless flow, but to do this we have to let go of our autonomous, separate self and fall into the Great Mystery, the Great River of Love that is all around us sustaining everything in being and reconciling all things. It is not that our individuality disappears. We truly become who we are, in and through relationships. The more universal we become, the more human we are.

The ultimate coincidence of opposites is this: that the God who is transcendent mystery became present as Jesus in our broken flesh in our imperfect world. He didn't come as a rescuer but as the meaning of all creation. He is the Word through whom all things are made, and he is the healing heart in which all things and all people are reconciled. As Jesus gave up his life on the cross with words of forgiveness, he became the Christ who is now present in all people and at the heart of our evolving world. This is why the Father created the world. It was the Jesuit scientist and mystic, Teilhard de Chardin, who spoke of Christ as the Omega Point, the end point of a Christ-centred evolutionary universe.

From all eternity the infinite God willed to love a finite other. The meaning of the Incarnation is revealed in the face of a loving, humble, vulnerable, healing and reconciling God. Whenever Jesus heals anyone, he always tells the recipient, *Your faith has made you whole.* For Jesus, faith does not refer to a set of doctrines. He is seeking faith as a relationship that believes and trusts the mystery that God is unconditional love. So when he visited his hometown and the people rejected him, the gospel records that he could work no miracles there. It is all about relationship and mutuality, giving and receiving. Jesus doesn't operate like a superhero, he doesn't force his power on anyone. He has chosen the path of humble, vulnerable love. He can be rejected, and still is in our world today.

We are here on this earth to learn how to participate in the flow of love between the unfathomable and transcendent mystery of God that comes to us in the intimacy of our lives, in the faces of the poor and in every flower and leaf of creation. This is the answer to Reg Dean's third question about the meaning of life, *Where am I going?* The answer is to live inside the evolutionary world of creative love that unites heaven and earth. After the example of Jesus, the new human is both prophet and mystic. The prophet engages with the material world and builds a future of justice and peace. The mystic enjoys the unifying life of grace as the infinite power of love flows into our world. Both prophet and mystic will eventually become one. When we love, God loves in us; when we suffer, God suffers in us; when we rejoice, God rejoices in us. This is the cosmic dance that Thomas Merton describes as God sharing his divine life with us. Don't think about it; just dance, just share the relational flow of love and grace that is in everything.

The Transforming Practice of Mystical Christianity

For much of Christian history we sought certainty in matters of religious belief. This was the period when the binary mind was dominant. Today we are increasingly aware that religion is more about mystery rather than certainty. Today, instead of fighting science, we are learning that in the quantum world very little is certain. We are surrounded by mystery.

In our attempts to understand God we are like the fish that did not know where the water was. Many of our Christian mysteries escape our rational minds: Jesus is fully human and fully divine; Mary is virgin and mother and the Trinity which proclaims that God is both one and three is the greatest of all mysteries. Our binary minds cannot grasp these paradoxes. That is why we need a recovery of mystical Christianity today.

At the beginning of his gospel story, Mark records Jesus telling us what needs to happen if we wish to travel with him. It is all about *metanoia*, a change of mind, a moving from our small binary mind into the Great Mind that is the Mind of God. As we saw earlier this demands an upgrade, a new software which changes the way we think. This is contemplation, what we have traditionally called prayer. It is not about what we think but how we think, how we perceive everything. It is the movement from the egoic operating system of the binary mind to the eye of the heart, which includes mind, heart and body and sees the whole picture.

The eye of the heart helps us to recover our true sight – so many of the miracles of Jesus are about curing blindness – so that we can see and participate in the cosmic dance in the everyday circumstances of our lives. Many, if not all of the problems that we face in our fragmented world today, as well as in our own families and communities, are rooted in the binary way of looking at reality. We divide everything into right and wrong, good and bad, carefully placing ourselves always on the side of the good and the correct. We love to say who is inside and who is outside, who is up and who is down, who is good and who is bad. Look at how Jesus deals with problems such as paying taxes to Caesar, responding to the woman taken in adultery, reaching out to heal the servant of the Roman Centurion, touching the leper, welcoming the good and the bad into his banquet, defending the woman who anointed him before the critical audience of men, dining with sinners and tax-collectors before the shocked purity-conscious Scribes and Pharisees. He also moved beyond the confines of his Jewish religion to include others, Romans and Samaritans. His Father was clearly not a tribal god.

We cannot eliminate our binary calculating minds altogether. They are necessary for many everyday tasks. But when it comes to spiritual growth we have to move to a bigger space. With our binary minds we live along a horizontal axis. At the same time there is a vertical axis perceived by the heart. These two axes meet in the now, and when we learn how to live inside the Trinitarian mind we can bring something new into the situation. Where the egoic operating system creates separation and division, the eye of the heart perceives wholeness. Whole-making describes the ministry of Jesus as he brought people together physically, emotionally and spiritually. He spoke of the Kingdom of his Father where all could live in a new unity.

What allows us to do this is a regular practice of contemplation. Like nothing else it breaks down the dominance of the mental egoic system. It opens up a reconciling third force which Christians rightly call the Holy Spirit, the Inner Witness, telling us that we are not just our thoughts and emotions. The non-judging gaze of the Spirit holds all things together in love. It is the divine aliveness and energy that helps us to hold the opposites together and bring them into a new creation. Our egos are not all bad; they are just not big enough to hold and reconcile the essential ambiguity and brokenness of the human condition. Unless we learn how to hold and accept that in ourselves and transform it into forgiving love, we will push it on to others.

Some months before he resigned, Pope Benedict XVI invited the then Archbishop of Canterbury, Rowan Williams, to address the Synod of Bishops gathered in Rome. This is what he said about the importance of contemplation:

> Contemplation is very far from being just one kind of thing Christians do: it is the key to prayer, art and ethics, the key to the essence of a renewed humanity that is capable of seeing the world and other subjects in the world with freedom – freedom from self-oriented acquisitive habits and the distorted understanding that comes from them. To put it boldly, contemplation is the only ultimate answer to the unreal and insane world that our financial systems and our advertising culture and our chaotic and unexamined emotions encourage us to inhabit. To learn contemplative practice is to learn what we need to live truthfully and honestly and lovingly. It is a deeply revolutionary matter.[36]

There are some who say that the mystical path is not for everyone. It may be that it will always be a minority choice. Be that as it may, I think that our twenty first century will see increasing numbers taking that choice. It seems more and more people are willing to practise contemplation. We seem to be reaching a critical mass, like a morphogenetic field, that will significantly alter how we experience Christianity. What needs to happen is the shift from the illusion of the separate, isolated autonomous life which has led to performance-based religion with all the emphasis on an insurance type of faith that will get people into heaven.

---

36. http://rowanwilliams.archbishopofcanterbury.org/index.php

It demands little transformation or growth and little need to get outside the egocentric mindset. I agree with Rowan Williams that contemplation is the key to the essential transformation at the heart of Christianity that moves us from religion as morality to a relationship of intimacy and love. All the mystics speak to us from this enlarged space of God's unconditional love, this place of acceptance and grace where we can stop worrying about our brokenness, our guilt and our unworthiness.

We can then accept and believe that Jesus as the Christ has pulled us inside the Holy Mystery that we call God, who delights in our unique humanity and invites us into the cosmic dance. In his apostolic letter, Pope Francis reminds us that the resurrection of Christ it not just a past event, it contains a vital power – love – that permeates the whole of creation:

> However dark things are, goodness always re-emerges and spreads. Each day in our world beauty is born anew, it rises transformed through the storms of history.[37]

The contemplative path is not an escape from ordinary life. It gives us a new set of eyes that sees oneness rather than division. Like nothing else it allows us to cleanse the lens of the egocentric, judging mind and learn to see ourselves, others, even our enemies, and the whole of creation as images of the beauty of God. Perhaps this is what Jesus meant when he spoke about the pearl of great price and the treasure hidden in the field.

Our modern connectedness was dramatically revealed to us when we first saw those stunning photographs of our fragile and beautiful planet from space in the last century.

---

37. Pope Francis *The Joy of the Gospel* (CTS London 2013) p.131

In a recent interview for the BBC, the commander of the International Space Station, Canadian astronaut Chris Hadfield, was asked what most impressed him as he orbited the earth from space. He replied that as he kept circling the earth he felt there was no longer any need for Us and Them: We are all One. Not many of us will enter space, but each day the gift of contemplation takes us into the sacred space of our hearts to meet the divine indwelling. In past centuries people found God in sacred places, stone temples and cathedrals. Today we are being invited to find God in the sacred space of our hearts and the sacred space of the universe so that we can see everything in a new way. As Julian of Norwich, the first woman to write in English, put it centuries ago:

> Truth sees God. Wisdom contemplates God. When these two things come together a third gift arises: the wondrous delight in God which is love.[38]

The story of science and the story of religion are beginning to converge in our time. They may use different languages, but they are both pointing to the same reality: that we all share the same history, and if we can learn to celebrate unity in diversity we can help build God's kingdom of love on earth as it is in heaven. We are all connected.

---

38. Julian of Norwich, *The Showings*, a contemporary translation by Mirabai Starr (Canterbury Press 2014) p.109

DON BOSCO PUBLICATIONS

STARTING AGAIN FROM DON BOSCO by Ian Murdoch
SERVING THE YOUNG by James Gallagher
KATIE COMES TO MASS by Kathleen Pearce
ROSIE GOES TO CHURCH BOOK and DVD by Kathleen Pearce
CHLOE AND JACK VISIT THE VATICAN by Kathleen Pearce
GOOD NEWS IN THE FAMILY by Kathleen Pearce
OUR COLOURFUL CHURCH YEAR by Kathleen Pearce
101 SAINTS & SPECIAL PEOPLE by Kathleen Pearce
TREASURE WITHIN by Michael J Cunningham
LET YOUR HEART PRAY by Michael J Cunningham
LOST AND FOUND by Michael J Cunningham
A TIME FOR COMPASSION by Michael J Cunningham
WITHIN & WITHOUT by Michael J Cunningham
SALESIANS – CONTEMPLATIVES IN ACTION by Michael J Cunningham
SEAN DEVEREUX by Michael Delmer
GOD OF MANY FACES by Sister Margaret Renshaw
MAMMA MARGARET by Teresio Bosco
SYMBOLS and SPIRITUALITY by Michael T Winstanley
LENTEN SUNDAYS by Michael T Winstanley
DON BOSCO'S GOSPEL WAY by Michael T Winstanley
JESUS AND THE LITTLE PEOPLE by Michael T Winstanley
BLESSED IS SHE WHO BELIEVED by J J Bartolomé

DON BOSCO PUBLICATIONS

TEACHER, TEACH US TO PRAY by Sister Winifred Acred
THE WITNESSES by Sister Winifred Acred
DON'T ORGANISE MY TEARS by Tony Bailey
BOSCO Z BOOK Illustrated Life of Don Bosco for Children
PRAYERS TO START MY DAY by David O'Malley
PRAYERS TO CLOSE MY DAY by David O'Malley
TRUST THE ROAD by David O'Malley
VIA LUCIS by David O'Malley
THE CHRISTIAN TEACHER by David O'Malley
CHRISTIAN LEADERSHIP by David O'Malley
SWATCH & PRAY by David O'Malley
ADVENT & CHRISTMAS SWATCH by David O'Malley
A SWATCH JOURNEY THROUGH LENT by David O'Malley & Tonino Passarello
ORDINARY WAYS by David O'Malley
WALKING WITH DON BOSCO by David O'Malley
SCHOOL ETHOS AND CHAPLAINCY by David O'Malley
MOVING ON by Margaret J Cooke
DON BOSCO - THE PRIEST, THE MAN, THE TIMES BY W R Ainsworth

We offer very good discounts on orders of multiple copies.
Phone **01204 308 811** or email **sarah@salesians.org.uk**